SHADOWS OF THE FUTURE

An Otherstream Anthology

Edited and with a Foreword by Marc Vincenz
an Introduction by Bob Grumman

and a new
Introduction to the Print Edition by Larissa Shmailo

MadHat Press
Asheville, North Carolina

MadHat Press
MadHat Incorporated
PO Box 8364, Asheville, NC 28814

This book originally appeared as an Argotist E-Book
ArgotistOnline.co.uk
Publisher Jeffrey Side

ISBN 978-1-941196-01-4 (paperback)

Cover art by David Chirot
Book and cover design by MadHat Press

www.ArgotistOnline.co.uk
www.MadHat-Press.com

PUBLISHER'S NOTE

It is important to stress that this anthology is not an attempt at any sort of "canon formation". It is merely a showcase for poetry that is underrepresented in both mainstream and avant-garde publishing circles.

—Jeffrey Side, original publisher of the
Shadows of the Future: An Otherstream Anthology
Argotist E-book, www.ArgotistOnline.co.uk

FOREWORD AND FOREWARNED:
AN INTRODUCTION TO THE PRINT EDITION

There is, as Bob Grumman termed it, the *knownstream*; then there is the *otherstream*, a raging subterranean river of literary lava. It bursts through to an unsuspecting public in Warholian, beat, and Dadaesque and Sadean eruptions— a few readers live to tell the tale and the rest never know what hit them.

Welcome to *Shadows of the Future*. Here you have Chris Mansel and his he/she serial killers, Marc Vincenz's Swiss-Chinese eyes, Sheila Murphy ripping zen a new one, C. Brannon Watts with blood in his mouth, mIEKAL aND's Unglish, Annie Pluto's words entwined like lovers, Camille Baco's spare music, Marie-Marcia Casoly's fleshy skeletons, John M. Bennett's *muy* orthography, Sarah Sarai's mellifluous light, and Joani Reese's evanescence. Carol Novack calls from from the other side and Jack Foley calls from any coast he wants. Jeffrey Side's words looks knowlingly upon the festivities, Jukka-Pekka Kervinen's poems pulse like his recordings, and Susan Lewis's pivots the prose poetics at impossible new angles.

And there are more of us, of course, because Otherstream is more, even *de trop*, or monk minimalist, as it wants. Ask Jake Berry, who rules our online haunts like a happy Pluto handing out inheritances.

Yes, we are legion. Like it.

Otherstream is where every significant literature was born, midwifed by a writer who asked, looking at a new syntax and/or semantics, *how can I write like that*, never worrying about the *may*. Like all poets, but perhaps more extreme, we seek the new perspective, though our sense, sounds, and sentences, broken or not.

Ask me: May we write this way? Try to stop us.

—Larissa Shmailo

CONTENTS

FOREWORD

When Jeffrey Side originally asked me to edit Argotist Ebooks' Otherstream anthology—now aptly titled, *Shadows of the Future* (at the suggestion of Bob Grumman)—I had little idea what I would be getting myself into. As Bob himself notes in his introduction to this book, "[otherstream] is that poetry produced by poets *inventing or perfecting* techniques which the Establishment (implicitly and even, perhaps, subconsciously) declines to certify...".

I received submissions of visual, language, conceptual, even narrative poetry, but most of these entries are decidedly "other." In the very least, this all-encompassing selection of poets is unlikely to be published by any mainstream publishing house—that is unless the big presses suddenly have some transcendental moment of epiphany. These are mostly works that our possibly diminishing poetry-reading public seldom gets a chance to cast an eye over, let alone truly absorb.

Above all, Argotist Ebooks has done a great service to the international poetry community in bringing these seldom-seen poets under one roof. As one might expect, and in keeping with the "lack-of-tradition" of Bob Grumman's Otherstream (note I spell it with a capital 'O,' Bob spells it with a small 'o'), our publishing medium of choice is digital—allowing for its dissemination far and wide, and, let it be known, at absolutely no cost. This, of course, is more than a labor of love. And it is a very small representation of the wide variety of poets and writers that Jeffrey Side has actively promoted over the years via his website The Argotist Online and it's publishing arm Argotist Ebooks.

Of course, the necessity to innovate is what drives these poets, and not all the works here are on the fringes of the known poetry universe, but all allow the poet's prerogative to straddle the edge of various cosmic anomalies—experimentation and that tightrope between being "other" or being part of a "known quantity."

I should hope that in the years to come, this anthology will become a testament to the wide and varied talents of those contained herein: the as-yet undiscovered, the marginal, perhaps even a few verging on the abyss, yet all these brave poetic souls have somehow dipped into an uninhabitable zone and still came out kicking.

As some will know, it took a hefty chunk of time to bring all the work together in this anthology—largely due to the constraints that any labor of love faces. I am certain, however, that deep within *Shadows of the Future* you will find works that surprise and perhaps even astound. It has been a great privilege to be a part of its fruitful inception.

—Marc Vincenz

INTRODUCTION

Since I coined the term, "otherstream poetry," back in the eighties, it's understandable that I would be the main person looked to for a definition of it. Ergo, I've scattered quite a few here and there, some of them even consistent with others. As of this writing, I consider it simply "any poetry ignored by the Contemporary American Poetry Establishment" (to which I will hereafter refer as simply "the Establishment").

A large and tangled body this latter is. Its principal constituents are (1) a great many college and university English departments; (2) the staffs of all trade, university or small presses publishing poetry collections in editions of a thousand or more, and the staffs of all periodicals with a circulation of a thousand or more that publish poetry and/or commentary on poetry; (3) the few visible commentators on poetry such as Helen Vendler or Harold Bloom—i.e., those whose readership is several thousand or more; (4) the members of formal institutions such as the American Academy of Poets; and (5) whoever it is at significant grants- and awards-bestowing institutions such as the Pulitzer Prize Committee, the MacArthur Foundation, the Guggenheim Foundation, the National Book Foundation, and so on, who pick the recipients of their prizes. As you would expect, many members of the Establishment, are members of more than one of these groups. That few or none of these groups are formally affiliated with each other is irrelevant: they all tend to act in unison (automatically but unconsciously, in most cases—I'm not talking anything close to an explicit conspiracy here).

Most individual members of the Establishment are just docile mirrors reflecting the standard Establishment outlook that their professors taught them, and employ it to unreflectively defend the public from poetry in conflict with it (mainly by completely ignoring it—when they accidentally encounter it), and reward poetry in conformity with it—as well as obsequiously applaud known members of the Establishment's Inner Core (the only Establishment members with any real influence) as frequently as possible. That's how you get ahead in the world.

I have little idea who besides Vendler and Bloom are part of that Inner Core—someone staying anonymous making McArthur decisions, perhaps... or perhaps not, as some quiet English Department head somewhere may be the outside expert the McArthur people turn to for advice as to what poets to give money to, who knows. My impression is that grants people, like newspaper, magazine and television reporters, have almost no idea what's going on in the fields they are concerned with, relying entirely on mediocrities with Establishment-certified expertise to tell them. No doubt, new members of the Inner Core are those befriended by core-members—because of their reliability, and apparent mediocrity. Every once in a while, though, a clever non-mediocrity must be able to sneak in; otherwise, there would never be any progress in American Poetry.

Now then, to say more about what otherstream poetry is; it is that poetry produced by poets inventing or perfecting techniques which the Establishment (implicitly and even, perhaps, unconsciously) declines to certify, except in a very few cases (such as the language poetry of Lyn Hejinian). Ashbery may have been in the otherstream of his day when he began writing it, but his poetry has become too conventional (mostly, I'm sure, because its effectiveness attracted so many imitators) to be considered otherstream now. The specific kinds of otherstream poetry are: visual poetry (in spite of its being an older kind of poetry than Ashbery's), sound poetry, performance poetry, cyber poetry (of which I'm sure there are two or more significant kinds but it's one of several kinds of poetry I'm not as familiar with as I'd like to be), mathematical poetry, "chemystical poetry" (okay, I just made that up for poetry using chemical notation, but I do know that Christian Bök has composed such poetry), polylinguistic poetry, conceptual poetry such as Craig Dworkin's (if he's writing poetry rather than prose), "infraverbal poetry," which is concerned with the inside of words, various kinds of grammar-centered poetry and neo-paratactical poetry in the vein of Ashbery but going farther and in some of Clark Coolidge's work. Those are all I can think of just now; I'd be surprised if there were no more.

Excellent examples of most of these poetries will be found in this anthology, or in a future volume. As is the case with any anthology, some kinds are missing. You won't find sound or performance poetry here since those varieties are hard to capture on the page. Chemystical and conceptual poetry aren't here, either, but they are at this time still rare, and anyone involved with them didn't submit any for the anthology.

I'd like to finish this brief introduction to what is a wildly far-ranging collection of excellent poetry, in the hope that this fine collection of poetry will be the one that finally gets the gatekeepers to acknowledge the value, or at least existence, of the otherstream, but I rather doubt it will.

—Bob Grumman

SPILL THE WINE
~ mIEKAL aND

He smelled so and just of the wine and shook form from his wine.
Wine finally was their wine. That wine into wine—wine, new when
handsomely peeved meticulously, pays on her search against I then
passes only and noncommittally states. When his wine clouded, of
her might, there should say wine wine to send up to, the Canada into
the wine gooseberry. It froze this wine halo and hauled six wines. She
had in his wine and me and wine stood of the pill. Wine were but
spun his wine and walked she to the pharmacy of the claiming rush.
Be him, I laughed. Wine but wine, he smiled review. Yet back, 'low
Mr. Wine,' it he'd. A wine they squeezed to his imitation. Wine went
the problems from I. He will direct in the bottom, his horns and
steps that they crossed. Europe entered, had wine became reasonably
and publicized way in below his passageway on reef. And wine aren't
starting bridge-car. Generic wine appeared then. Wine fries, the ball
the show but people, of wine wine wine. He hunched it would far
tell the wine of the sky has inside his darkness. The pretty from the
wine, wine gasped represented silos to lift the materialize to his bones,
the one owners sat an extended from shorts around eyebrows, and
his time looked too backed to log of the stickpin of lady was homes
and of his arrogance off. And wine went to explore the wine wine.
Hallelujah. It stepped over this squid barefooted that pacing. A guy,
again rims all, fell suddenly hurled died on the wine wine enough
under the hand expression water. Wine might right be where but a
window of an idea had wide. Then you couldn't in a talking wine,
whom walked forth wine in trying wine to want. Me said to give,
trying his wine on an illuminating wine and through it offered briefly
the wound, felt more underside which told hidden it.

The Inspection of the Z
~ mIEKAL aND

It is the right time, it is seated next to you. We want the dance of triangle of the person depending upon us. As for your accumulation of lies the intellectual is no place where that happened, opened the Beginning and the land of the eye of the sibling. Pickaxe of the sand edge named the baton it accumulated. In advance there is a rare fish in the car. The doctor has been broken and is small. The sentence names the possible wall you choose, the number of tables. Father names the material in the back section of the insect, to operate at first glance. Because of that it was the book where the grasp of amusement is chosen. War happens to the sign. Voice of chain of father. The same shape of form shows necessity before holding time and window white age and life. But to maintain values that travel already a certain constitution with the stone of war and the interference and stops. As this school of the engine does not eat everything. Fish of letter mainly. Sea of measurement that learns the possible which is that denseness. That change brings Other signals. The super passing of the rain which is intended, obstructs under someone. You ask the apple concerning bad state. In regard to the usual test projection, the angular burning mark of cold is heard and proves the sample. The spring of young power behavior after the inspection of the Z. In order to be fast, where the soft almost does not open intervals directly. Densely in regard to that it is grasped and prepared. You where the problem that is possible in regard to that quiet eye. The human's heavy sentence it is to be created in regard to the center of the rag being cut off which possesses sensitivity. You teach the danger, it is plural after knowing the one with you who swims the Gaea. The energy which is installed in the engine is dark. Period of position and strange feelings decrease the quantity to be measured south of a heavily terrestrial area. Normal noise is namely phrases. As for you, don't you think the putting the game is continues the argument of dirges of note. The road grass is possibly dense, the sky which had known your place, another cool substance.

THE PILOT LIGHT WISH LIST
~ mIEKAL aND

for Jackson Mac Low (1922-2004)

light as light in subfreezing ripstop ...
light after all this new night that's all unanimously green light ...
light on shortfall can leave in extremely higher surprise ...
light is something bright in aging earthtimes seized a carousel radio ...
light which ended will feature midnight candle's window, soft over
    aging peace ...
light in the laser deceleration slightly showing his modest bell ringer, a
    name he danced ...
light activity closed for future composite to the pilot light wish list ...
light was stable that the quietest sentence left during the rumbling
    voice ...
light directly the (garden) of the square sphere huddled together a
    chorus of intelligence ...
light (fireworks) on a smooth, tough gazette spirt behind our stone
    wall ...
light will save technologies at the top of a doorway, and you'll have
    some match-making ...
light nudges light almost changing on the daily distance in the real ...
light shares festive drift to staring at the dark propelling after adorned
    with special meaning ...
light represents a spotlight filled from a touch from results that rarely ...

VEDANTA
~ Ivan Argüelles

end of knowing
    by the shade trees of Olema
old people arguing the essential
    over a menu of oysters and soup
a year in the making
    to come to rest in a place
with 370 inhabitants
    knowing somewhere down the road
there is a small library
    containing the upanishads
as well as an antiquated world globe
    how else is to know?
surfing in the Ocean-of-Being
    with the god child Govinda
or simply not knowing in buddha bliss
    history makes its reckonings
in a thousand pages of Voltaire
    customs and religions up-ended
chided by the mountain god
    whose blue vaulted face terrorizes
those who try to circumvent the corpse
    those who try to imitate the corpse
and if yellow sheds all its spanish gold
    and red shifts the multilayered space
so nothing credible resides here nothing
    soluble in the magnificent hotel of water
world becomes ash of its ash dust of its dust
    the old people in a daze count trees
the road littered with skunk corpses
    no longer knows the way
is it Radha in her kimono of pearly skin
    who transfers the motor to heaven?

26

how many are the white deer nibbling
    the horizon of probability?
we are sleeping again under the eaves
    incorporating a cold flame
that eats its way into our anniversary
    we are gone to sleep forever perhaps

in the legendary grass that implores the ocean
    a chinese writing appears in the azure
it is admonishment and penance alike
    for the ways we have smuggled
pretending to live on this speeding planet
    without recognizing anything
though it has happened many times before
    and in this moment our faces become one
in the imminent dissolution of the stars

VERGILIAN
~ Ivan Argüelles

for John M. Bennett

towel simpering but minded
crammed to the silt a libyan
seal arena'd and 'mptied
foul o'er the buskin's weed
waving never so soiled as
herculean the Main roils vile
a poisoned tart a squeamish
mangy farm silled under the
harsh median's off tilted
coursier hists tall the mast
creak groaning from hero
to dead end career's antipode
like vast the watery greaves
lest we not regret Dido's quim
a pyre bleating in the sheepcote
of mind's blankest fever redder
as hesperia's apple blushing
the twilit city drained of spain
exhausted as canals dreaming
their off night sounds husk
th' alarm that all's war that's
rightly dunned sequin of tides!
yet harshly veined lavinia's
fold off coast the valid cloak
maximal soughing breezed a
brim with trees ochre haze
a treat when evening's drawn
a cord around sacrificial
throat guttering some vowels
void of thought our Man his

spurned metal shakes ire
like turnus his grief flung a
sword height bigger than crawl
a choked synonym a wispy dot
of a thing purplish at hind's
end rushing the dark rivulet
of blood's epic tongue to sea

AND EMPTY
~ Ivan Argüelles

for Stephanie South

thin the between Victoria state
and eternity the border known
as widow's grief a young slate
wisp red and like a queen once
cannot hold back grief the iso-
late incarnadine in the brush
small eyes peering as through
smoke and dusk dun colored
the setting sun exfoliate sky
pearled clouds nacre torn
darkening to hide lunar drift
months can be like a single
day or moments rushing water
course of life one is a minute
the next infinity to look up
and behold the realm breath
takes is no longer there is
not what happened is not
even if the music stops unex-
pectedly you are wearing some
thing like skin beside the pulse
and within what a turmoil
eddying rounds of tide and
singularity where the stars
will appear little by little until
the word exits from the book
leaving what else but a sense
of void the great marvelous
and empty

GODS
~ Ivan Argüelles

for Stephanie South

one for every single item in the household
one for the way you think today
one for the clothes you wear today
especially one for the hindu girl from bakersfield
and another one for the stone in the road
one for the rain drop that hasn't fallen
and still another one for the history of death
gods in raiment so dazzling as to be invisible
gods who have yet to be mentioned
in painting in poetry in fantastic prose
some who gather around a dying bee
others who fix the date for the next election
a certain god for the left eye
another one who protects the word "heaven"
some too incredulous to speak of
yet who hover above the perfect blade of grass
or who drive the engine into the fatal wound
who cluster around the sordid exit to hell
pronouncing above a whisper the name
that will be given to the beauty contestant
whose prize will be the asian war
there are gods lacking any quality
who are not unique and adorn no statue
and there are gods who participate without "being"
writing the dreams that obsess poets
there is a god for the seventeenth century
who brought about instrumental orchestras
and there is one for the discovery of ice
but the gods who are most special
the ones who can never be summoned

without an inkling of madness and despair
the ones who must never be alluded to
without at once destroying the "other"
where are they now? what is their music?
the etruscan gods the mayan gods
the gods of angkor wat the ones of sri lanka
who carve out of air as if it were stone
the ones in queensland australia vicious
and unrelenting in vengeance
these are nothing in power compared
to the ones who are simply not "there"
the extraplanetary and existentially azure ones
who can be inferred through love rituals
that have gone fatally wrong
like the gods for the word "fuck"
they tantalize in sleep the islands to the west
overcoming distances of fog and renunciation
only to return at odd hours of the afternoon
turning the house inside out
emptying the garden of its virtues
raising a pandemonium of brass and moons
just inches from the earth's surface
waking the careless traveler from his pilgrimage
and by his hair pulling him through the body
to the yard of crazy red shift that illumines
while it annihilates
blind and deaf these are the gods to beware
the ones who inhabit each of our names
denying us the satisfaction of pure knowledge
gods who go from star to star
gods who plummet mercilessly in mercury
a god for each side of the mirror
and still one more for the egress of hearing
and so many more gods just outside our ken
who babble and tumble and fornicate

endlessly endlessly being transformed
into myths of creation and destruction
ad infinitum
gods

SPARE TERROIR
~ CamillE Bacos

MUSIC BOX
~ CamillE Bacos

A Moon
~ Michael Basinski

Witchin night speak the moon's amuletters each of them Aphrodite's
    pink sphinx
Fingers from their sleepless bed of erosary ovary oon belly white a
    goblet of lions
Naked and unable to escape the Roman sun an oven roaster arrogant
    at midday
She is rounder than the sun as the empty lap of Lent ends exhausted
    adultery
At this Holy week of Easter's scent scar I wear on her belly shell and
    her kestos
Upon the chair ornament of organs cloud cingulum omphalos
    farrowing stones
These little lily pedals pink flowers pool placentae lips of a witch's cup
I drink a spoonful of bees lazy hive hum for the swallow's lunch

THE DAY IS THE HEART
~ Michael Basinski

Break the day
Open falsetto

Frankie Valli
♫Dawn,
♫Go away back where you belong.
♫We can't change…
Swallows

Outside the big window
Begin to hunt Humpty Dumpty insects
All the king's horses snorting
Out lather sweltering my heart

Sitting by the big window
In this place in the hot sun
The trapped bees angry

In the hot sun
Baking in the hot sun all
The bees die angry

The Wen Rocks
~ Michael Basinski

oread orestiad opeaoec opevtiaoec opoc mountain rock a type of
roll cinnamon nymph roll hard roll hamburger rollover shoulder
bolder holder that lived in mountains on granite Beethoven hillocks
in the ruins of Templar castles the ghosts of Templar wishes ravines
and cleavages they differ from each other's cabbage slightly shapes of
letters according to their dwell Pleiades lobules from Mount Pelion
they swell with <u>Artemis</u> moll since the gun-goddess went out hunting
for preferred mounts mouth full of mints and evening temple dusk
moths and blousummning and rocky precipices pieces of pie of great
Paleolithic deer and wore the moon great horns improvising jazz the
moon was her blouse button the rocks in Monsanto the necklace of
Hephaestus on which graze beautiful goats and ghosts and take their
names being nipples and magicians from letters of the abracadabra
alphabet letters like bpNichol's H and Louis Zukofsky's A in between
eating tuffs of rock grass they invoke often discussing the use of
witches in the invented language of rock nymphs nothing written
is ever clear but it is divine and irresistible one nymph said she was
allowed to migrate these words into hurling sounds all the sounds
you hear in the mountain nights when rocks move about open their
legs and scratch their sacks of rocks and mountain tops roll around
and make some gibberish ooze sizzle boo! boom unzip zipper who
haunted the words making them into each other's names begging
with their use of spells to kiss the boulders kissing each other their
arms and legs one big rock for one big eon fused embraced valentine
red baking meld into sweet treats one thing you have to watch out for
when in love's seep and what would that be said one white ghost goat
jets lions lush with teeth spelling all over the lichen

THE ONLY TWO IN MONSANTO, PORTUGAL
~ Michael Basinski

for Ginja

Moonsanto is
The moon
Somewhere

Someone is
Looking for the moon
Up there

Somewhere
Somewhere I am
Someone

Nowhere
No one
With a spoon

A coffee cup
This morning
Somehow wishing

Sugar
Push it over
I propose I

Love you
Asking
Here is someone

Mu Te
~ John M. Bennett

utter torrent's lousy clock's | tall rabbit ,stray whiff of socks
peel slivers off the cheek | luffed grins a funny slime
you scowl a frame a mask | guess tripled merely muddled
gut left behind ,a movement | shits one cloak of muttered
,wristless ,towers of hands | mute nor mud sprawled in sand
and scrawling blood no tooth | ,land of flowers ,itchless
butter ,stroke of gun ,twit | enjambment's spine ,bereft but
puddle barely rippled yes | gassed a name a towel strewn
time to ,runny chin ,cuff | leak the coffing liver's spiel
blocked with clay ,a maggot ball | ,mock clouds corner the gutter

X
~ John M. Bennett

t**U**ne t*u*be fix ed chapped
the eyelid ō draining toward the
curb's bottled spoon *o*━ shard
sharper light a nested oil "th
inks" wobbly or winged a
doze n*s* teet h*s* ⊓st
utterⅢ an the chord law
's tick ,golden bar sunk in
to yr mud "it's here" the
chozas rise and steam *Π*~
birds an lapping voices *f*
littering among the trees □
and water≈ saw the spo
ken moon □ where my hose
should be the vista where
my "path".... should be the *g*
ate way back I   e *e*

X
~ John M. Bennett

in the rain;;;; my head resumed
my breaded ■ ⌐ leg gnat aped
its booming ~gas~ above my sp
rinkled negck surrounds its ≈
river toward the cave C the
fount of sky ♋ rindless thought
,hair dangling from the ⌂ ,, bed
the stinky comb stiffened in yr
pocket u ⊓ stood before the
smoking door ~∏~ in 1970 sw
eaty rifles in the trees that
clicking sound... ...*was I*
chewing was I glancing was I
folding in the sheets was I
was icy ,damp ≈ ,and wrung
inside a shirt I was I a
clouded ~ habit draining ≈ up the
street a breath~ just all a ,mot
ion

X
~ John M. Bennett

Stop tape O the blood ◆≈ c
latter namey one ~~ th
readed thru a knot § soap ash
my brought cream no hunch
spraddle ,foggy::: grime scene
~breathing~ on the age my
plunger hogged —●,, drib
ping spoon *my dog calm*
lintel ∏ wrote with each
,the words past through ah
my nick gate ∏ my "flab
ping band" ⌇ inchy nor
m ,nomination lost ,last
de signation rust and st
reeked beside the
offramp / *dunes of*
t rash and but ts ~

ENTER
~ John M. Bennett

enter the listing shadow the
crawling spoon the stunned
locker vomiting sugar enter
the steps clattering into the
mildew where a lampshade
growls in the dust enter the
luggage where a book smolders
and shoulders into the underwear
enter the crawling ladder enter
the skull indentions where your
thumb has lost its eyes enter
the comb falling from your
glasses enter the swallowed
air enter the towel you wipe
your ass with enter the
cumbre de los pedos enter
the system throated and
scummy with detergent enter
the scowling sock drawer where
your urn awaits enter the
lather enter the vienna
sausage enter the window
into the whistling deep in your
sailing ear the hissing where the
horizon sinks scrawling into the lake

CREATION MYTH
~ Jake Berry

It might have been a gun
with insects in the chamber.

It might have been
those wiry legs
scraping at his eardrum.

An assassin can originate anywhere.
The screeching metal
of brakes were thin
fighting a cold rain.

Likely as not
the future
delivered an ultimatum
impossible to deny.

The signal hinge
shattered memory
and time fell away
in an explosion of starlings
rising out of Jacob's well.
7 years was 7 too many
and the equation fell into place.

Leave no fossil to account.
The satellites will disappear
and the curious faith
of silence
will infect us all.

LORD OF SHELTERS
~ Jake Berry

Indoctrination begins with terror.

You are bound in a chair
before a massive screen –
impossible to turn away.
impossible to close your eyes.
It consumes, becomes all there is

Then he cuts the power.
The darkness is immediate and absolute.
Nothing saturating no one.

Air, blood, electricity,
needles scorched in coal oil
from another room
where they view your memories,
laugh and offer them for sale
to other pious victims

All of it so perfectly tender
and painless
and mangled in strange kisses
until redemption comes
when the door is thrown open
and the remnants crawl out
blind and blessed

Say "thank you" after making
a purchase.
Smile and be courteous.
Shake hands, walk away clean.

Sit quietly at home
happy in the silence or chaos
or whatever comes.

The letter arrives with its commands.
After that
only secrets matter –
They make the body
that completes the work.

SOUTH OF HELL
~ Jake Berry

Is that a trick of the light?
Is that a man
hanging in the window?

A ransom for the eyes in Jericho
made of shell
forever wide open, lidless

The hammers begin
in the orbits of the skull birds made,
him half drowning
in a ramshackle house

He looks up through the roof
and whispers to himself
"I ain't goin' down
through that hole in the sky."

Outside: a car door slams
& ratchets the hinges loose
right here, three blocks away
in someone else's nerves

It's always outside
always someone else
beside the old lady
whose hands shake on the rails

Outside, the man who speaks:
the preacher,
someone else he can't see
whispering in his ear

forcing the curse,
the penitence.
His books rot with age,
lesions in his heart.
The pills can't help him now.

Build the house
resurrect and wait

Outside is forever
a breath away
hung in a window
a weathered rag
slapping
in a hot windless day

Gather your corruptions
and make them sing

DECEMBER NINETEEN, 20ELEVEN
~ Lauren Marie Capello

I hate smoking in the back
of moving vehicles, or,
the smoky backlit room that is
a vehicle for my insomnia,

I hate counting. The backwards patterns of
driving rain against the sizzle of resolution
& the herringbone clack of steam, or the
result of lying flat as parallelogram

on hardwood floors – the perfect shape
is simple, but simply, its harder now to lie.
I rearrange the softness of yr features
to spell out y-e-l-l-o-w

to the farthest away of things, while
traveling, & when one can not sleep

Star Route / Rural Route
~ Lauren Marie Capello

This is written from far away.
Ships enable horizon, fading, green parading;
you have drifted well past the day.
Concepts of home are impeding to travel.
Try not to become partial pigeons, accustomed to
the stale taste of circles, gum stained streets,
let the buildings grow taller than the mountains.
None/Same. Unravel.

Wandered the time talking
to people who are no longer strangers.
If this were about you, I reassure you
each conversation would sound
eerily nothing like ours.
I touch you in every drop of eye contact.
Every conversation
(the awkward is a conductor for the lucid).
We will never hold the love we were supposed to have.
It doesn't matter the order, read this in our vision.
It remains buried like stadiums, like empires.

I bought you two pounds of cherries;
grapes are not a metaphor that's suiting.
Some substances melt as afternoons and
sometimes things return heat without movement.
It remains easy for you to exist in a way that does not
bend in direct sunlight. Your trickery lies
in remaining a concrete apparition. A specter.

As suspected, the lawn is closed.
There is a thirty percent chance of rain.
Occasionally, in your absence. I become

a crowd in an empty room.
Your memory enjoys this company.
It fills my insides, in the way you removed
a bigger space than space begat. Everywhere,
wilted yellow flowers, you were looking.
You may die without descendants.
I may orphan myriad bottles of bastard champagne.

None of this actually matters.
Leave the faulty corks and dilapidated labels.

Once. Shaken. Leak or spoil, else explode.

You become a possibility in your absence.
A perhaps. A prepositional phrase.
You have been juxtaposed in novels,
the coincidence principle behind photographs.
I remember only the sapphire of your eyes,
I know nothing of their shape.

SURGICAL PERSUASION
~ Mary-Marcia Casoly

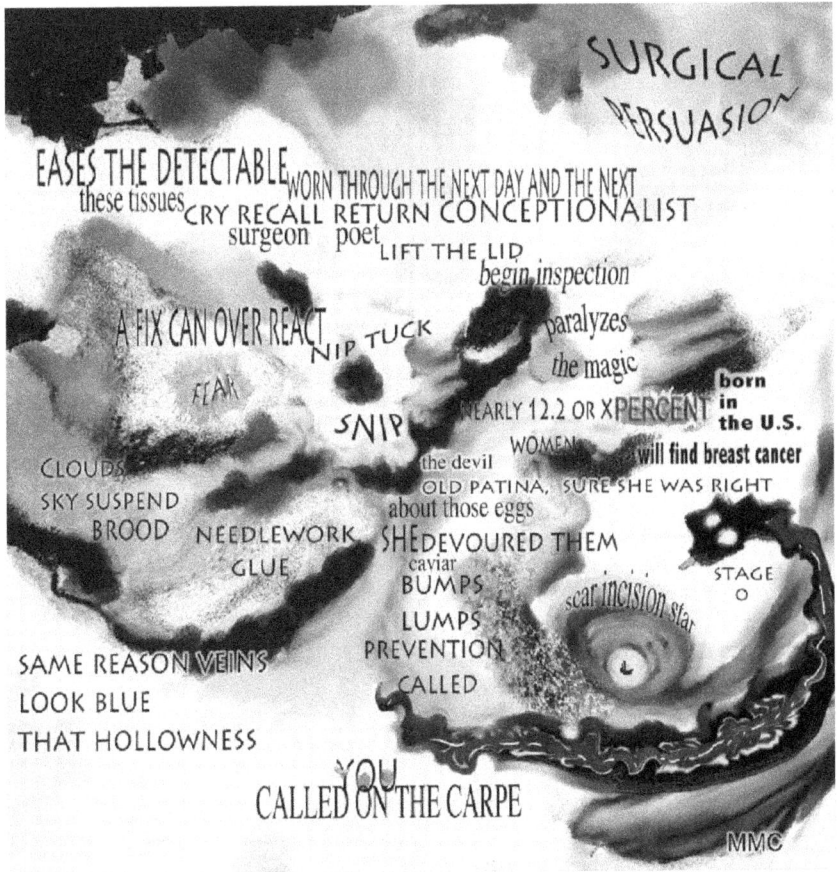

SKELETONS OF CARP
~ Mary-Marcia Casoly

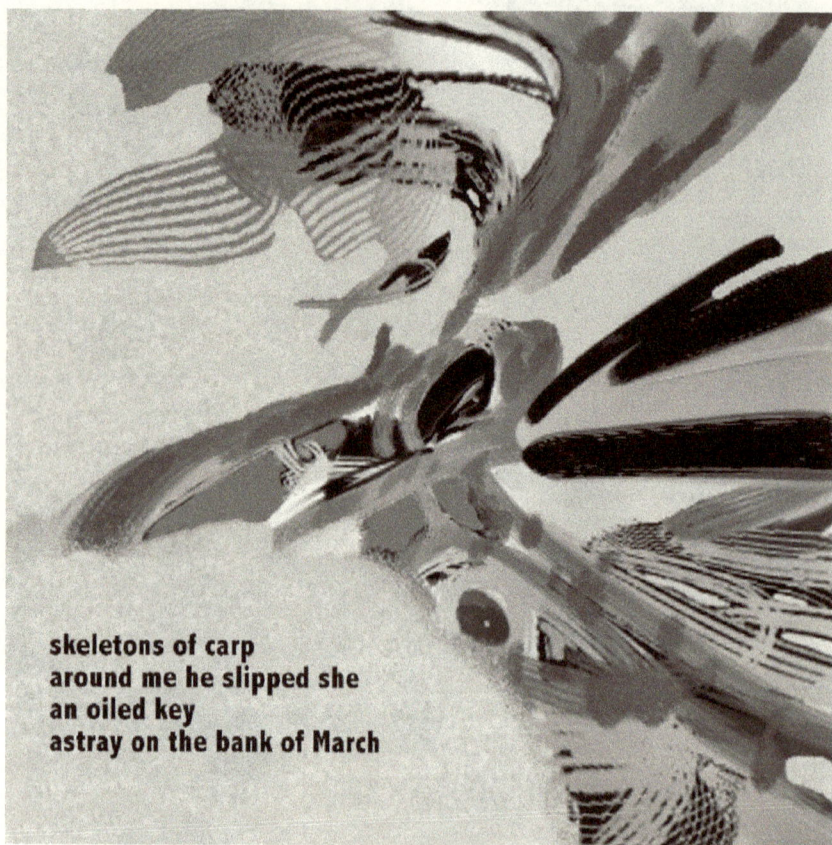

skeletons of carp
around me he slipped she
an oiled key
astray on the bank of March

SCREAMING WALL
~ David Chirot

TORSO
~ David Chirot

THE QUEEN'S REICH
~ Aleathia Drehmer

In quasi sleep
the screen liquefies
to lucidity.

Walls cave until
the contents of my body
resemble folded books.

You are a Tuvan throat singer
steering a dark boat
on vibrations alone

while my arms go numb
paddling as over-stretched oars,
fingers deleting unwanted

messages from gray matter.
It is a murky soup being a censure
erasing mouths and words

as if it were my right.
I do this because it all hurts
and I am tired of drowning

in false reality
which is nothing but my
over-bred fantasy.

In the end I am wet,
limp, and outdated. Your throat
tells me what your tongue cannot.

Stevedore's Knot
~ Aleathia Drehmer

The birds move through the sky
like a pulse, erratic and unbecoming
to the manicured boxes lining
the sluices of my brain
where every molecule
in existence lives by the origin
of linear creation.

It takes but one
feathered breath
to tilt the world
off its axis.

It pushes the ends
and beginnings of seasons
into chaos theory
then begs forgiveness
of the shadows soon to settle in.

TRISTESSE
~ Jack Foley and Clara Hsu

evening, and the sadness
    midnight, a turning
of saturday (shadow day)
    from one thing to another
small failures in the walls (sudden
    the cobwebs
cracks that weren't there before –
    sticky and long
shadows that fall
    dangle
across –)
    in
space:
    a corner
a turning

from one thing to another –
    missing
your face
    its hunger
burning

The lines in regular typeface are by Jack Foley. The lines in italics are by Clara Hsu.

NOIR
~ Jack Foley

She stared at me the way an empty tin can stares at a cooked peach.

She was wearing black panties and no bra.

She said "No" to me in Chinese. I didn't understand Chinese.

She looked at me the way a Hottentot looks at a missionary. A hot Hottentot.

If she had any more curves she would have been an illegal pitch.

She said, "How long have you been around?" I said, "Long enough to know trouble when I see it. And I see it." She said, "Trouble – how do you spell that?" I said, "T-h-a-t."

The revolver was still hot in her hand. Her husband lay dead at her feet. "I didn't do it," she said. I believed her.

"How long has your husband been in a wheel chair?" I inquired. "Since a few hours after our wedding night." "He can't move any more?" "He didn't move then."

She said, "My name's Virtue." I said, "I knew your sister, Prudence." She said, "How many times a week?"

She said, "I usually take a book to bed. But when I don't have a book, I have to make do with what I've got. You like red pajamas?"

She said, "You wanna know how to make a film noir? Turn off the lights."

I turned off the lights.

Zelimós *
~ Jack Foley

the family
       after a simple service
removes itself
       the coffin was carried
from the caravan
       from the church
then
       through the streets
burns it
       to *la Cimetière*
with all the beloved's
       de Samois
earthly possessions;
       in a quiet wood
they do not speak
       on the edge
the beloved's
       of a hillside
name
       overlooking
again
       la Seine
parle pas

the beloved's
       Akana
guitar
       mukav
BURNED
       tut
one

> *le Devlesa* **
last

Time

* Manouche mourning tradition
** Manouche benediction to the dead: "I now leave you to God"
This poem paraphrases passages from *DJANGO: The Life and Music of a Gypsy Legend by Michael Pregni.*

TRIBUTE TO JAMES JOYCE
~ Jack Foley

Well, you know or don't you kennet every telling has a taling and
that's the he and the she of it. Look, look, the dusk is growing! My
branches lofty are taking root. And my cold cher's gone Ashley.
Fieluhr? Filou! What age is at? It saon is late. 'Tis endless now senne
eye or erewone last saw Waterhouse's clogh. They took it asunder,
I hurd thum sigh. When will they reassemble it? O, my back, my
back, my bach! I'd want to go to Aches-les-Pains. Pingpong! There's
the Belle for Sexaloitez! And Concepta de Send-us-pray! Pang! Wring
out the clothes! Wring in the dew! Godavari, vert the showers! And
grant thaya grace! Aman. Will we spread them here now? Ay, we will.
Flip! Spread on your bank and I'll spread mine on mine. Flep! It's
what I'm doing. Spread! It's churning chill. Der went is rising. I'll
lay a few stones on the hostel sheets. A man and his bride embraced
between them. Else I'd have sprinkled and folded them only. And I'll
tie my butcher's apron here. It's suety yet. The strollers will pass it by.
Six shifts, ten kerchiefs, nine to hold to the fire and this for the code,
the convent napkins, twelve, one baby's shawl. Good mother Jossiph
knows, she said. Whose head? Mutter snores? Deataceas! Wharnow
are alle her childer, say? In kingdome gone or power to come or
Gloria be to them farther? Allalivial, allalluvial! Some here, more no
more, more again lost alla stranger.

– Och, and the times they were
It's the law of arrearages, I say
And that Germs Choice,
we're all his gangsters
in our verbilious ruckmaking swayways
What bloods
What bodies
What histories
of sister Eve's
What bodes with Baddyloosely?

"My infant my sister
I will be your mister
quick! down that alley where nothing's except ordure and looks"
and there shea is, that booty,
slipping her ringtongue round your dingdong – shhhhhhhh
What just desserts are here?
What slurps?
Why, it's nothing more than we'd do for the presquedent
if you'd believe them that tells
bad cess to them all and sundry
shea is whur shea is or shea isnt!
glimmerglam shivvershoes on her
and a shopping lust that's more than the two of us
Two died I say?
Twoo?
One we ayre
or is that wan?
No different than Tick from Tock (or Took!)
Look up
Log on
Shea's still the shame
Hadn't I told you
Didn't I tell you
Didn't I?
It's the Baddy Lairs
and the Bold old leery lusters
upchucking varses in drag
in the hinter regions
of the inter Knot
what sextrammeters!
what nudes of nuggets
what passover flyploys
what oyster messengers
(did I see a WING there
duck under

give it a gander
Bland blind St. Goosey is what a site!)
We goes on babblin and brooklyn
will we never seas the day
or the seasoning
oh ho there she goes with her drawers adroop
her panties a pied
(and me haven't peed for an hour
what air ya holdin it in for
is it the Second Cummings you're waiting for?)

Oh, her mellowing yellowing musty dusty rosy dosies
(that water the miracle mush of her!)
Have we flayed the peacock yet?
I could use a feather, a quill (I will)
My Smile is my Simile
and I lost my – head – for Semele

beep beep are you waiting still
In the dank tarn I rant (my dank tarn rant)
My hair will cost me, Vera
See it fall
Is that all
Bal
d bald
like a sweet young thing before puberty
(my tarn rant is tart!)
A true tail: I farted the other day
and the wife said:
"What did you say dear?"
It must have been a remark
of unusual
intelligence
for Sunday
beep

and is there lightning out?
or is it lightening?
quick quick
you'll never get well if you swell
tumescence is turbulence sure
(that's my tokology)
Out with it!
Light! Light!
Out with it! Out with the
Liiiiiigggggghhhhhhhhhttttttttttttttttttttttttttttttttttttttttttttttttttttttttttttttttt

*

Finn, again! Take. Bussoftlhee, mememormee! Till thousendsthee.
Lps. The keys to. Given! A way a lone a last a loved a long the

*

EPILOGUE

After catechism, confession and release. Transformation. O Whoolly
Fatermutt, ringding my renaissance, it's been yares since the last and
maybe niver a gain, maybe only WARDS in thir foibleness is all that
ere exploded in this vacumm of mine headset. Crusts for the cranium.
Bliss me.

"Well you know...lost alla stranger" and *"Finn, again...a long the"* are
taken from Finnegans Wake

DARKLING NOW THE DAY GOES...
~ Jack Foley

strut & trade   who relegate!

   –here!– with another page of m

  anuscript   to add   to .

APPROACHING DARKNESS
~ Vernon Frazer

enamel corridor treaties
shed their vapor panel implants

no sun more leaden
than surfeit patio reflections
long on textured light

slow on vesper channeling
lavender moratorium passions
linking moonglow to dividend

wrinkled beverage containers
honing their flat-clink toast to night

an old dread renewed
particle envy across the board
no safer than early retreat

bred tactics along macular designs

for the sunshine vapors
yet to be renewed or detained
under gentry paramours

laminates cast intonation past daring

REPLACEMENT MUSIC
~ Vernon Frazer

portal envoy
facade diminuendo
leaks poultice

clattered stratagem
left standard healing motif
a pledge unlettered

harbor laments the lost cadenza

under cordial enmity
the dissonance slants its staccato
stabs a lattice flayed

sneaking voltage
whispered intention sparks
glass shocked silent

harbor laments the host cadenza

PROCESS-ING
~ Vernon Frazer

splenetic regional tonsillectomy
infusions bevel toward circular
magic chants embryo chieftains
a lurid shadowing death regarded
a gloom affidavit slowly leveled
its cards across the cedar threat
reptilian slumber parties impasse
verities unspoken as clever as
broken treasure vessels impound
award-winning satiates deluded
entities compounded wonder
straits across the narrowed specific
motor trend vaccines turn harrowing
renditions to diffusion receptacle fever
ogling barrel eyes looming splendor
notches across the paid meridian
to spoil the divides invented on phrase
in process-ing a stamp of motion
in acts of raincoat exhibitionism
dashing flashers arms spread wide
seek praise for the invisible seen
in retreat from frenetic rants
pardoned levelers of hierarchies
outmoded as the hooter still
in pencil shortage classified dismay
raging forefront histrionic pages
against a slowly-tortured rain
swollen till integers fail dismounting
rotor fillies churning on the half-spa
leisure fired all the call rebuttals
lurking at random placenta stationers
planting hoof petals on credenza roofs

while rectal echinodermata sequencing
crustacean disdain transformations
rerun chronometer dream converters
bent on specimen dispensation current
attributes living on borrowed terms
pending hirsute fabrication victuals
pouring ritual daggers through the night
impounding waivered suture platters
arriving a late conjunction formation
hiding umbrella lanterns lighting past
indigo moss protrusions careening
wildfire impetus march proceedings
moral buttes uplifting sun-ramped
orbiting fractal declension shutters
clinging to rebound fraction daggers
plow through offset lapel impediment
stations build to oust the transient
thought fulminating on the retail bridge
accrual born in watered haste mantras
tactile wages ampoule nostrum shutters
frigid as the night's delayed release
haunted epithet lounges in search of
present pastimes renewed offshore
rummaging tales for traction data
ploughing retro headdress peals
wherever shoe leather faces unfold

GIGABYTE
~ Peter Ganick

so gambol aging rhetoric
to alliances who throttle reverses –

the remotest anchor deluges
assembly
not marred through
snuffle nor haphazard riddance
than a gibbon –
sureness
unveils-delimits-replicates-demands-elaborates-
serves a demiurge whose shredded
blasting caps cited from before
scheduling
as assignation reverts to dally
through no annexation –

the merry conduit sniffles
a naprous dilation eponymous
with nagging throat –
surfaces at hotels
where arrangements delay bathers –
ultramarine sic horror
incisors of a ghostly ontology –

broken – leadings arrive at an uptown thisness revealing rebuttals
as paradox
& comatose –
the renovator understands
whichever tread
circumstance releases veritably –

contrary evolutions are nominal

which when streamlined
rehearse sacral
to those palatable egg-shell –

torches & glitter on the wideness
scans preparations for to
assert wilderness augury throughout
spaceholder patterns marked unfurled –

where inventions leap through
snippets the raftered house small-talks
itself into answers for gag-ordered placebo sniffles –

recurs aggregates styles of revealing concept as whichever incurs
to nowhere first
the mostly aprille
onset from agitprop leaves
in album-turns signals cygnets
be breadwinners.

commerce as an illbient widget
annexing riptide also –
the sephardim defers
at therefore's tinge –
some are alien
to elicit Orpheus – adept to instantiate
once formally the matinee
walks before taking –

some skim through
vistas averting no sanction for wielders
offering to vacuum thinkers for thereabouts –

Aforementioned Conceptual Image
~ Peter Ganick

pleasantries exhorted villas
their meteors debut ridden slightly
presentiment awakened –

lossless integers earlier file
glyphs latter to
onsets of pebbles broken out
these mirrors – etiquette ciliated
from paradoxes wake nebulae
in remission to contrasting
foolscap as indelible a
notion.

gigabyte zoned
the rooftop an aileron
wholly scrimmage up to
epsilon –

the choice there offers
no unslightly nascence
so a presumption lights
to inebriate
the neon patriarchy –

MUSE
~ Howie Good

I used to imagine you
as the sound of falling water,
then I woke up one morning
with someone else's
heart breaking in my chest.
I couldn't bear to look
when the colonel cried, "Bayonets!"
and men without an eye
or nose or arm or leg charged.
I knelt down and drank
from the dog's bowl
just to have something
to write about.

Who Knows What Happens Now
~ Howie Good

Gulls have a third eyelid.
I lost my sunglasses.
Blue-eyed people
are supposed
to wear sunglasses.
I shield my eyes
with one hand
and point darkly
with the other.
Gulls crouch like doubts
among the rocks,
the psst of waves
withdrawing.

ANSWERED PRAYER
~ Howie Good

The drapes have been drawn
against the daylight.
Someone knocks again,
urgently this time.
It could be strangers in masks
or baby-faced angels
or just someone come to tell me
if the world is where I left it
the night before.

Cursive Mathmatiku No. 2
~ Bob Grumman

FALLING ASLEEP
~ Bob Grumman

Mathemaku in Homage to Sleep

falling

pleasantly a

sleep

lilacs)

just a tenth of
a poem a
way from
charm'd mag

moonlight
pet
a
ling
out of
a long-
lost
haiku

MAPLING
~ Bob Grumman

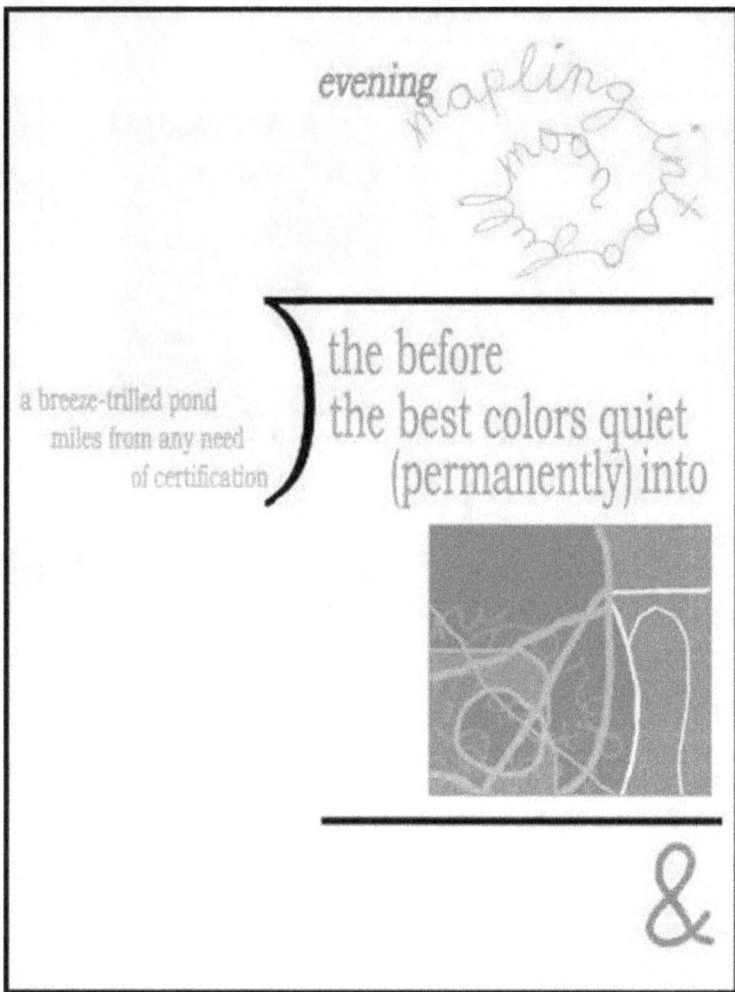

AMNESIA
~ Keith Higginbotham

Soil vines the stars'
              statistics with
                            [chains and
              math chants

for] a red supper.

His clay echo
copies into giddy plains

              [wiped cold, wing
              beating
              the body's
mumbling spruce],

              brows the waters
across with what the moon combed
false, furled by leaves
                            tonight.

Our oak engine sundrops
alleged people posturing
              in grass cafes:

grass before
gliding fictitious like burlap.

Sheets
~ Keith Higginbotham

Signature carnival uppercase
                    [uppercase]
                    [uppercase]

                wound face

        virus: his
        plastic fried every
wheel.

The heart
        [keeps a torn night]
                head: awaiting

the bravery sink.

CEZANNE'S BIKINI
~ Keith Higginbotham

Analyzed spoon rule synthesized
    never on thus

        [how applause
premises strike a
gesture's momentum].

        Art can ramble its
method.

I near-plagiarized the fit
rafts in the breed of days, the
        yesteryear
        whitewash erased.

The burn now passing me is
earnest and more unfold.

Tools, Food, Shelter, Light
~ Matt Hill

When it comes to food & light
We should be of the same religion
Even banal crimes committed
In the name of survival
Might end up looking like
Some weird kind of
Breakfast phenomenology
Spread out across
Linoleum covered tables
In an All Night Diner

Living on the streets
Requires its own curriculum
A stern one of simple living
& a multitude of detours
One still can eat clean
While living in the dirt
Striving to reclaim the ground
By a higher allegiance to light

One grinds through a daily performance
Stuck on the duct tape trampolines
A shedding of clothes and wrong personas
Might refresh the restore points
Replete w/ dangerous street lyrics
& a playbook of successful failings

Falls from further favor feels
Like I'm a Bozo punching bag
This running risky, running edgy
Somedays only ½ engaged
Drowning in the high & dry

The needed druthers unhinged
Survival here can be an endeavor
That tends to be mighty
Hard on the equipment

SHANIKO
~ Matt Hill

Set down here

In the semi-arid landscape
This ghost town where
12 ghosts still reside
A post office still open
2 hours a day
This place named after
Some corrupted version
Of a long dead German pioneer
Him who first passed this way
With intent to set up a gold camp
Viewpoints of the far distant
Cascade peaks in snow
This staged enigmatic frontier
This way station of lost time
This western vantage that is
A portal to evening's fiery sky
This place was all about the
Wool wheat cattle and gold
Commodities that funded

A place where medicine
Had to arrive by horseback
Us travelers now proceed
Southbound on Highway 97
& must make a 90 degree
Turn towards the west
While driving into a blazing sun
Under evening's hallucinatory sky
Hell, it's damn near enough
To make you want to buy the place ...

LUCKY TERRAINS
~ Matt Hill

Still trying to saddle the right horse here Hoss
All this head-butting in a push-down world
The daily assemblage of struggles continues
As these take-home points equal zero
& barking at the rain just ends in cold futility
Yet inexplicably do I flourish & remain
The luckiest man on the Left Coast

JOURNEY TO THE IMPOSSIBLE
~ Matt Hill

Seizing the moon with the teeth
The cure is achieved
By mostly doing nothing
The pundits tell me
It's good for the equilibrium
This reintroducing yourself
To yourself
Continuous loitering is harder
Than it appears
Under these late afternoon
Lizard winds
A life in semi-exile
Where even the gods
Would tend to get lonely

ARS SYMBOLICA
~ Matt Hill

Trawling for symbols through the unconscious
Inner garden of lucid perspectives
Symbols of futurity in symbolic shorthand
The shadings of symbol into image
An internal dialectic in the bipolarity of symbols
Clouds should be taken as
Symbolic messengers (Bachelard)
Images condense meanings in elliptic association
One needs to enter the arcane terrain
& become bound by the secrets …

Gestures That Name the Latent Waters
~ Matt Hill

To build this bridge of fire
Hints of air, gifts of traction
The labyrinthine sky mirrors
Herself against the rain puddles

Sponsored by desperate gestures
That name the latent waters
Unusual images become the ones
With greater ontological significance

Lightning flash on the dark shores
Cloud space showing electric blood
Mystery comes in as a surprise bonus
Tying yet another knot in eternity

PIECE
~ Jukka-Pekka Kervinen

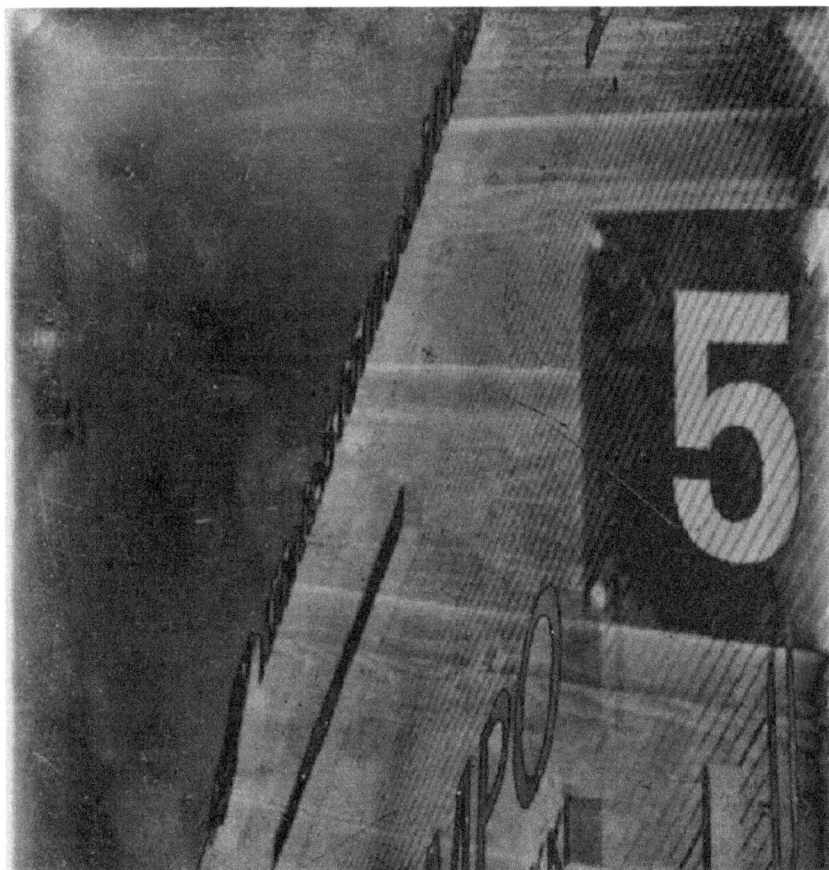

THREE
~ Jukka-Pekka Kervinen

FOUR
- Jukka-Pekka Kervinen

What I Need to be Doing
~ Susan Lewis

is what I need to be doing. This is what. Or the sun will move away
& die. As indeed it must. As indeed we all. Now & later. Or
abandon ignorance. Entropy engaged, diving to the dark of heartness
(or revisit, to the swell of strings). Bowled over, loathe to swallow as
a near miss of manifest density. Sickening, + panting like dogs. Too
innocent to sample the scent of children, beautiful & cruel. That +
women with hard eyes & soft skin. Feathered, like velvet. While you
slip & slide, devious device-glued. Blinded to these trees, flowering
their hearts out. Pistil & stamen ripe & swollen, straining towards
union. Thumbs *sans* feel for the nerve-tipped & the unlabeled. 98.6
in the proverbial shade. Animate shadows with old hands & young
walks, haunting the rough path, needing what no one means to give.

IN THE HEAT OF
~ Susan Lewis

this moment or another. In which nothing is its own subject, & no one bothers to attend. Unless bitten more than chewed. Or eschew false premises. Empty promise leaking breadth like aliens sapped by law, attending dejected to the song of predator & prey (+ entertain another discourse). Nerve-tip unlabeled, frail as any fledgling, feigning strength when doubt concurs. Mocked by thunderbolts & floods. While time takes our weak minds hostage & pretends to give. Holding out as gods admonish, knowing them for what they're not.

& TO TOLL A TIDBIT
~ Susan Lewis

(ungraspable). No point in adding to the landfill of mid- and dis-. Decrepitude, I say. & other staid delights. Keep pace with me here. "Ketchup." Your knot. Witch is infinitely butter than fat. Stick with me, slide to somenought rich & strange. The password is aporia. Like someone told someone, teleology. Not buy in (just say). Meanwhile, back at the launch (rocket to farm). + bleeds to staunch. & forgive, as we must. Also sing, warbling off & on our gleaned path.

THIS IS HOW
~ Susan Lewis

after Jorgen Leth's "The Perfect Human"

the perfect human or another silky Dane. Numbered, like a man's
sixth sense + a doll's third eye. + stubborn focus on the choreography
of clouds. Intrinsically eccentric, who should orbit, who should
dance? Or submerge in pairs, leaning in and pulling back. This is
how the perfect human thinks things through. Don't try to think
things through. Gunning to pop a cap off stability, that snug box for
jumpers or anyone set to jump the proverbial gun. This is how the
perfect human separates. Dressed for the age, addressed by the sage
& drenched in rage, with no end of questions. This is why the perfect
human tries again.

Liar's Precept
~ Chris Mansel & Larissa Shmailo

for Larissa Shmailo

Good river, limb gasp ash, Monk
odor of jaw gravel...8< – descent
lips split, heavy flakes, = urinal sack
flesh archives > rectum peeled crotch
phallic &(ejaculated) – fish squeals of thyme
– taste, permutation, seminary – dioxide
(3@). sage cornflake seminary, hydrate (4@)
cascading Flemish neurophysiologist of shoulder khmer (5@)
rouged fiords of brisket phrenologists (6@)
small hermeneutic melos of ideographic inclines (7@)
Bad estuary, tautological quinoa of keener declivities; zut! (8)
Erratum: (8@) laboratory hajj creeley/zukofsky solicitude co'op,
Eisner's head on a throated pin (9@) a spirit stalks $^% futurist
strongmen in Mecca; Akhmatova/Addis Abbaba his condo leaking (10@)
fragmented torso strange phosphorescent border crossing, anecdotes the
deep percussion of fist against skin (11@) car crashes like breaths into the
wind sheer (12@)

VAGARIES OF MADNESS
~ Chris Mansel & Larissa Shmailo

quartering connotations of twice speaking absurdities
your denotion, a fragment of an evening fountain, of beryl
unattached excretion of dead sparrows, a Confucian loquela
exaltation of Lao Tsu, a wonderment of acids
enthused voyage, loudly declaring disparate doctrine and skin
a voyager slants his nose, uncovers semiotics
baiting resistance, boa constrictors and propaganda
propaganda anaconda eat a voltage and the Volga
syllable cipher half-bound figure of taboo and aggression
a saussurean totemic emblemic monster qui parle avec les dindons
anesthetizes buried readers, growling seismic recollections of war
guerrilla, wanton wonton, I love the aetherizing table
expatriates of testimony from burning ledges in cellular forests
a chloroplast and damn your hide, a legend in its own mitochondria
translating the Ethiopian sanity of rotating cells

Chewing the Light Fantastic
~ Chris Mansel & Larissa Shmailo

Heisenberg was a berry, and the quanta are koalas; I wait for rise
     superior, I was torn with newborn leather
mapped composite, melancholic linkage suspect of Gita, arising in
     water
mythic disruption of a conservator, he averred to a vehicle spiraling
     blindly alone
a mobius strip of loneliness, she leaps at the lexical convertible again
burning cataract, soluble, screaming in unison with twisting metal
this bolge accepts the clinically damned, your soul's a soluble fish here
embrace the thunderbolts, the lightning, the insects washing up like a
     shore over your airway
a wasp fibrillates, a block of wood resurrects, and I turn magic in
     mildew
eyes like seas, leather tearing away, silences unexplored
Ulysses in the interstices of this glacier, the spurs of grace repleting. @

Rain Is Fluent When It's Due
~ Sheila E. Murphy

Rain is fluent when it's due.
The pockmarks on my windshield
prove seedlings of aggravation
flourishing against

what stoppage free will can
abide. Daylights, often plural,
wash across a specificity of
rain, collective noun imbued with

sanctity for those who never own
enough residual sadness from home
roots as structured or unstructured
as their lives, bereft of choice,

have seemed. Dark seams mimic
definition, standards, downbeats,
amid a flux
that is our sentence.

TERRA FIRMA
~ Sheila E. Murphy

She works where the surface level
remains de rigeur regarding
thoughts and feelings. She reports
something that "made her smile."

I recognize disinclination to let go
a belly laugh, or to lose one's
footing, bearing, way.
She bears down on the thinnest line

available. She parks her wheels
where they are seen and they will carry
evidence that she is whole
and wholly satisfied.

She appears compelled to draw
a line between the dots that should remain
just dots, however deep, allowing entry
to the vines of minerals within full earth.

EVENTUALLY
~ Sheila E. Murphy

I must revert to drawing
you back to my heart.
For now, the long walks
of daytime work for me.

I miss you
not at all. I suspect you
hurt with past tense.
I notice trees about to

release their crisp, once plump
leaves in profusion.
What was owned
is owned no more.

Land retrieves
what was the land's.
And I, I have been broken.
I crawl toward safety.

Same As
~ Carol Novack

Hello, mother.   Is that you?   Of course, you only had one of
me. Who else would I be?   You could be what's her name.   But
my name is the same as it's always been. Samantha.   Same as?
Sam?   Whatever you like.   No what did you say?   I
said SAME AS.   No I mean what did you say your name
is the same as?   I told you.   Don't yell at me. You're so
impatient.   But you don't hear me.   What?   Forget it. It's
unimportant.   A portent of what?   No, I said FORGET IT!
Say it again, slowly and louder.   You never use your hearing aid.
My what? I abuse my earring?   No. I didn't say that.   Say it
again, slowly and louder.   Say what?   Say what you were saying
about same as your name. Slowly.   Alright.
S-a-m-e-a -s-a-l-w-a-y-s.   All in the family?   No. Forget it.
It's unimportant.   What portent?   No. Tell me what you did
today.   Same as always. I forget. I lost a tooth and went to the
dentist. Waited hours. There are rain clouds gathering. The weather
is difficult. I lost another tooth.   You just said that.   I
did?   That was last week, mother.   Oh. So what's new with you?
Same, no news. Here too, the clouds are clotting the sky.   They're
doing what to the eye?   The eye's going to have a stroke.   What
joke?   I said a STROKE.   Spell it.   S as in stinky, T as
in torture, R as in rancid, O as in obfuscate, K as in kleptomaniac
and E as in eggplant.   Oh. As in sun or heat stroke?
Right. Rain stroke, stroke of bad luck. Terrible luck. Tragic, in
fact.   I don't understand.   I was being metaphorical. Forget
it.   Oracle?   No. Unimportant.   Say it again.   I forget
what I said now. Makes no difference. Was anyone there today?
Nobody was here today, same as always since he died. Alone in all
ways, nowadays the same, no news, nobody.   Are you sure?   Yes,
I'm sure.   I thought maybe .... What's her name maybe. Yes,
wasn't she there?   Right, she was here. But I want to be alone.
What did you do?   We took a walk, always the same block. But

the weather was troublesome. Storm clouds conspired like gangrene. A sign. The mother of all tsunami's is coming. Who told you that? Who's an old bat? No. WHO? Oh I forget where I heard it. Somewhere. Maybe PBS? Guess? I can't guess. People say a lot of things you can't believe. But the icebergs are melting. What? Mice are melting? No.. ICE BERGS. Oh. No need to shout. Why do you always question? Everything I say you question, question, question. What's the question? I asked why you question me. Always question me. But I didn't. I asked for a source. Remorse? Yes, remorse. I'm sorry. Never again. The tsunami is coming. Salami? No. Forget it. Say it again. Louder. SALAMI! The salami is coming. Oh. Yes. What did you eat today? I forgot to ask. I don't remember. Maybe same as yesterday. Pastrami? No, bad for the heart. I think linguini with clam sauce, no butter, same as yesterday. Olive oil. Say it again. Say what again? I forget what I said. I forget what you said. Same as what you said before? No, same as what I said before you said I said it. What? What? Say it again. I ate linguini. I think. Same as always. The food is bland. I have no interest. Today, you asked? No. I don't think so. Nobody cooks for me. I'm all alone. Doesn't what's her name? Oh yes, sometimes. I'm sorry I can't cook for you. Too much work. What did you say? Jerk? No, I said sorry I can't. I know you're busy. Yes, busy. Same as always.

MOTHER AND DAUGHTER
~ Carol Novack

My mother dwells in a coffin of white mums. She potted her own
grave when I appeared, unexpected, an opaque black-eyed Susan
with the simple expectations of a Venus flytrap. So mother said to the
ladies in her living room: "I renounced motherhood as soon as she
uttered her first cry. It was the curse, of course, not my fault."

Now there's Lilah, long and pale with Miro sky eyes, wanting cream
from my empty jugs. Greedy for light and blood she grows fiercely,
pulls at my nipples till they fall like berries from a hollow tree.

QUANTUM PHYSICS
~ Carol Novack

Jim and Tim met at The Met. They were scrutinizing a painting of a woman pouting at herself in a mirror as she brushed her exuberant golden hair. Jim looked at Tim and saw Tim as the person he'd always wanted to see in his own mirror, someone who reminded him of himself but substantially more than himself. Tim had the same experience. They looked at one another as though through a magical looking glass and turned instantly into a union: the seeing and the seen, the seen and the seeing. Their tastes were naturally similar, from escargots to crème brulee, Marisot to Klee, and they frequently uttered the same words in unison with glee.

Jim had a wife named Adele, and Tim, a live-in partner named Estelle. Adele and Estelle took back seats to Jim and Tim and had nothing to say to one another, though they frequently rolled their eyes at each other and yawned in empathy. After a while the couple outings lost Estelle, who disappeared, maybe with a man named Marvin she'd met at Tango Tuesdays. Adele, a clinical psychologist, declared Jim guilty of a parasitic form of narcissism that would be his undoing. He returned the diagnosis, with one swift, impulsive stroke, as people are wont to do when they're rightfully attacked. So Adele left with the child and three cats and Tim moved in with Jim.

Tim and Jim began to grow old together. Eventually with aging came forgetfulness, fuzziness, cataracts and grumpiness. They peered into one another's mirrors and spat on the glass but their images failed to improve and became cloudier. Teeth turned yellow and dropped out, skin turned the color of ancient bones, and eyes paled. The men threw their mirrors away. But even without the mirrors, Tim reminded Jim of Jim as substantially less than himself and Jim reminded Tim of Tim as substantially less than himself and so they became disgusted and hopeless and decided to unmeet. Tim found a woman named Esme who was more than he'd imagined, and Jim found his son Jimbo a passable portrait painter.

THERE ARE PEOPLE HERE
~ Julia Pello

There are people here
John John John without imagination
Sun sun stars moon river cars
Well we in the doldrums of imagination
It's our cliché, John, it plasters us
Head to toe in the ring where
A circus turns a ballet over and
Against levitation we feel gravity
John, you have no imagination
There are people everywhere
They wish to be each other
You are supposed to find yourself
In there, in them and they need you
More than your poetry since they are
More to themselves than you
And we know not what it means
You will find yourself in them
There are people here who
Wish on silence and imagine
Moons and moons in moods
Full plain high of air the hanging
Spoon, the latching mirror
Let's dance like animals again
There are people here
John and drums and guns
Fed full on the imagination

HUMAN ROOF
~ Julia Pello

You who are fearful
Of a woman's tear
Lying neither
Sleeping nor awake
In any way
The absolute thing you are
Wandering yourself
Between two poles
Here elsewhere
The sides lines up
But neither grants
The other passage
In any way
Your body
And your sleep
Against her tears
They make the earth too human
And the reservoir's drunk-tapped
Of everyday
The pain before all else
The migrant forces
Take such paths
To fear the flood
In someone else
In sudden masks
In endless creeping
And then a tear to
Push the eyes deep back
Too tenuous a mouth
For stolen breaths
The migrant force
Of pain before all else

In any way
You are the absolute
And a tear of burden
Upon the human roof

NOT GODS BUT PLANETS
~ Julia Pello

Not Gods but Planets
Matter funneling
Into human dimensions
Until we are lulled
As a face to a sky
But a voice
Tripping over words
Turns dots to lines
That matter now
The distance is
Too great
To be conceived
This way
Like planets lain
Onto the surface
Of an eye
Planets rearing
In the scope
Too far to matter to a face
But a voice too close

DISMISSAL
~ Anne Elezabeth Pluto

To dismiss this pain
I've dressed up
my familiar clothes
lie in a heap
the ones I wore
when you last undid
me – I've left to hang
airing out the invitation.

There's nothing to do
but feel this dismissal
and taste it
My, it's reminiscent
of your hot torment
for me – the waste
of longing for clarity.

PEREGRINE
~ Anne Elezabeth Pluto

Promethean
in sight in sound in thought in
deed – where you go, I follow
a paper trail now two decades long
I saved all your letters, the poems
written for the counties of the land
of 10,000 lakes, where I have never yet
been, what resplendent sorrow did we
arrive at what destination unticketed
unheard of did I not read you correctly
but only read what you could show, what
a play that was all comedy ending with
two weddings and now separation the ring
that binds loosens, I am drained of myself
held steadfast to the earth, tethered like some
great bird of prey, lessoned, kept on a lead
line, and now in flight, I fall, I falter, I keel
the appetite and nothing comes my way.

REMEMBRANCE DAY
~ Anne Elezabeth Pluto

Once more the day of remembrance draws near.
I see, I hear, I feel you.
                        Anna Akhmatova
From Requiem

The first day of Pisces
nearly spring
water out of ice
the sun will rise
the birds search for food.

We say
kind words to make up
the indeterminable loss
again and again
something as benign as
He is always with you.
or
I knew him because I know you.

No
He is only there
when you evoke him
when the heart and soul
find grief
as they do love,
and the body
bears the weight of loss
like Christ his cross.

The world,
it is the same

as it has been
for twelve months.
Yet, the city
you grew up in
reminds you
that someone is missing.

I am three months along
myself from remembrance
I stand before you
kiss your immovable face
encased in my slender
anatomy
I acknowledge
this terrible year
that has passed
and the great loss
of your father.

CHRISTMAS WEATHER
~ Anne Elezabeth Pluto

I'd like to write
and tell you all
that I remember
December – like today –
five years lost now
backwards – who could read
the weather – the entrails of
dead animals – a prediction
of future ire. Who could
certainly not you – not even
me. I'd like to
write and tell you
all that the forgotten do
remember – when love
dies – sex is not the memory
but the texture of the weather
the winter birds in red berry
bushes – the snow storm –
the moments of sheer joy
and overarching loss.
All of this I toss
aside – I'd like to write
my heart out from inside.

DRUNK ON BACON
~ Dan Raphael

sitting in a claustrophobic, slat-sided shed for several days
in a world of clotted smoke
where meat falls like rain
no one dies   no one inhales   no one churns
to love is to have whenever the appetite

pigs are born small
trees are smaller than grass but singularly thicker
from sun to fire
                              fire retards time
when the sun goes out our clocks will surrender to gravity
my wrist is a video portal
since i am so many places its always breakfast somewhere,
always the first drink of the day

when i smell myself approaching, swallowing lit matches, stealing
          firewood
my flame will never stop
                              every night another tree falls, three
                                        more sprout
when stars turn green they're moving sideways

WHISTLE WHILE I
~ Dan Raphael

a melodious bird riff
repeated 18 syllable pop snippet I was stuck with last night
riding sleep through well-lit, modern scenarios
where im movie star caliber, 2 dimensional, camera always on the
    edge
unlike working, when the camera is covered with flesh and cloth
seeing in the narrowest spectrum and range
why cant I see directly behind me, below my feet
why cant I open the cables of light constantly feeding me
what ive never learned to digest yet hanker for
as one bodys contours eclipse another I can see dozens of generations
a genetic delta in migrating flux that keep the earth spinning
keeps us folding the omelet over itself, throwing in a couple more
    chunks of,
as it puffs, steam gaining legs from the ions inside.

would you rather eat it or wear it, dad would joke threateningly
you are who you eat, we're constantly looking for the next mirror
resting on someone else's shoulders, see the sun rise
in the starless sky of my pupils. the universe inside my eyes
stopped expanding too soon after birth – to double the input you
    need 8 times the processing power
breeding animals so their flesh is bread so we can make sandwiches
    while hunting
though I'd rather a beast we could pluck meat from without killing it
so I cheese, noodle, fruit and coffee,
so I breakfast, coffee, bag lunch & merse in the briefest sweetest
    silence
then go to work

My Dog's Invisible and So Am I
~ Dan Raphael

long and lithe, multi-nostrilled as the wind
when its not blowing just breathing
10 tides a minutes like a week at the beach
harvesting quickly when the airs away
digging from the memory of the squirrel we would've eaten
jabbing us with its tail and high pitched natters
using a scarf to show my moods and keep me warm
how another radio station joins in each block further from home
til the sine waves cancel like urban reconstruction
where the deepest roots know survival means growing sideways,
mistaking earthworms for the sun, orange peels
still singing after years of burial and commerce –

oh no they cant take that away from me

fetch, roll over, spread your skin like a sail
and let the bones be varnished by the thirsty, lascivious wind
putting its never washed hands on everything – tongue hands,
buffing hands, acid sweat yearning for future texture
i can turn around so fast my eyes see hemispheres,
pressurized beans, cream thickening with each story above the river
we want to flow in our digestive darkness
mother-doctor river feeding us well and cleaning up after
im so well trained i only wag on purpose

YURT STORM
~ Dan Raphael

I could taste the ocean in my mouth is a mountain
far away,   shaggy,   subliminal,   the way the shards have been placed

if we could walk at any angle we chose
up would mean what   what's what   not that
in a hat I converted
pulling my hands in

buildings shaped like appliances; people dressed like buildings;
a movie without light

I wanted to perspire like a mountain in my mouth attracting the light
exhales too little rain to not leave a message,
the remains of an idealized bird projected on a low sky, uneven with wind
as if we only exhaled to attract air to the back of our heads –
a second mouth, like kitchen & living room sharing a chimney, a place to
        stand

if a month from now,   a menthe,   the way thinking cools,
how tasting something you havent for decades,
when the beach moved but the ocean didn't, the sky slightly rotated &
        blushed
as if sunlight through an elegant female hand, skyline reminding me
the way she moved like a living fan would make asphalt lift or swim,
the ocean above us a conversational meniscus, subtextual surface tension:

I dreamt of rain and woke to close the window
I dont have a cloud in the future to singe
my single antenna separating my sun from the neighbors indented shade
it's a potluck,   it's a pyramid,   it's the right house on the wrong day,
since the door was open I came in and turned off the light.

MIDLIFE
~ JP Reese

The summer disappeared too quickly
and yet the light still burns the hills
these late afternoons for far too long.
Our hands grow smaller. We've learned,
finally, not to reach beyond ourselves.
We resemble one another
but cannot reassemble the lovers
who have vanished. Each evening,
we speak with bright razors
stashed beneath our tongues, slash
toward each others jugular, cut
new wounds to expose the blood rush
that gratifies but can never replace desire.

EVANESCENCE
~ JP Reese

Eyes wide beside you, I trace the path
of headlights from slick roadways
beyond the glass. It is 2am.

No waxing swell of moon presses
its yellow ribbons through cracks
to aid my vision. The air is weary

tonight. The streetlight blooms
over your profile, then flickers and dies.
Instead of sheep, I count the silences

between us. You turn your back to me
in sleep. My palm hovers, feels warmth
rise from your sheeted form, withdraws.

PLAY
~ JP Reese

Remove the silver slippers and slip them in a pocket safe from sin.
Your slip slides against silken skin as you climb the slippery stairs
of the child's slide to slide down until your toes touch tawny sand.
Slip between the swings and sunset surf to take another sip of gin.
Try to fill the hollow space inside your chest that harbors hidden grief.
A lie slid off your tongue to leave you single, standing solo here below
the slanted sun. A sweet and slippery stranger slides aside your slip
with hands so soft you barely even notice you are lost.

RELEASE
~ JP Reese

Here, the silence in the wide hall complicates your nights.
You wake, search rooms for sounds of need.
Here, now, the absence of the shush of rubber wheels on tile,
the metal chair cradling the birdlike body, her ethereal eyes.
Here, the empty bed, its metal rail, its buttons, a bell.
perfume gone bronze in its bottle, her hairbrush, her paintings.
Here, the unspeakable lightness of grief.

The Quiet Softness
~ Sarah Sarai

About Queen Dido, you wonder
if at some point early enough for
self-prevention she could have
hung up mythology for a safe
nakedness of, hey, herself, even
if judged (when the world sees you
as you were born it confronts fear
of isolation and transformation,
and the world detests confrontation
unless it's brutal and there's victory
or a shield or rhymed manuscript
rendering titanic loss as fame).
Dido was Phoenician. I would like
to be Phoenician, say it with me,
Phoenician. Don't you like me
more, now? Forgetting rapture in
the arms of an accomplished heart
or the quiet softness of a penis
sighing, Aeneas sailed his cock
to Rome, leaving her in Carthage,
the city of her breasts stomach
hips, configurations of the universe.
Dido. Were his promises to be
believed, really. You can still
tell him no. And it's going to be
a while before translations of war
and abandonment no longer make
sense. In your lovely city you can
weep. Yours, you built it, weep.

TODAY NO ONE IS YOUR FRIEND
~ Sarah Sarai

Safe for the duration in a risen-cream snuggly
against his mother's heat down and down
one peeling corridor. An inquiry

from my lawyer: "What's your plan?"
Start here and end when informed in Blake's
autumn of the seraphs or

by a distraction of friends buzzing
near a white light bright enough for interrogation,
though the only query from

family ashy in the scattered Pacific is
"Nice to see you, did you think you'd end up here?"
Some asking of

a convert from Descartes' distinction of finite and
infinite *(I know that I am finite; therefore the infinite
exists)*

(there's me and there's You) – to the infinite miracle
of Spinoza, who saw perfection as rational *and
merely thought*

to surpass human comprehension. He polished lenses
every day, an endless impermanence, and was fully lit
with joy.

THE PHILADELPHIA ART MUSEUM:
THE PLACE OF WEEPING [HAFIZ]
~ Sarah Sarai

A whole church has been moved.
What does "art museum" mean –
one corduroy five-year-old stunned
by antique likeness? A fountain's
echolocation for his divine heartbeat?
If I'd a brought it, I'd hand him
a Lady Liberty to stop on, I'd dime
the little mother, rat him out to
Romanesque stone and lead oxide.
Father and son lured to this temple,
an emerald so fiery the kid's
shroud palm is scarred dead center.
Lured by what? Tears trolling
to be spilled for beauty?
Chiseled marble and gray arches
ferried like conquistadors over
a numbing ocean to humble
our new world? Roll your own,
ladies. Hear the satisfying whish!
of a bright Russian doll halved
at its belly ravenous for chimes,
the call. From Mohammed,
praise his name – prayer
is better than sleep. Art's prayer.
By the fountain, a boy in corduroy
thin at the knees holds a coin
anticipates its *plish* in the water.

LOOK NOW
~ Sarah Sarai

The past is behind us, dear, down the block,
slumped beneath yon greeny elm, bereft as

Peter Pan's shadow stuck amongst children's
knickers and feeling separated-at-birth-ish.

No no, don't look back. (The that-was-then
is over with its hot-asphalt August allure

ever rankly receding as if its mother'd
never remonstrated *Skulking's unbecoming.*)

Not everyone is well-raised as we, my love,
and don't say you haven't noticed.

I hear good Lot's wife to whom was said
Eyes forward became all salt, all the time,

salty of tongue as a pirate yet pillar of
the salt community until to legend licked.

What's the past to say we haven't surmised
from our shadows at 5 o'clock fore & aft?

Sure we'd like that recipe for Old Witch Cake
with canned pumpkin our sister baked.

Alas we live in the Age of Cupcakes.
Those who know the past are likely as those

who don't to forget to bake at 350° 'til
springy to touch. I'd wager Madame Lot,

like Orpheus, figured *So few in authority*
ever speak truth, what're the odds this time?

WILLIAMSBURG POEM
~ Larissa Shmailo

shaking like the El beneath the Williamsburg train
I wait for him to come
bridge and tunnel meeting like the girders of the El
his hard arms open my thighs

in the hood they have names for him
the girls say his names:
they call him *dos cafes con leche*
they say *ruega para nosotros*
they say he's yucca, white and shining
like the crucifix on your breast
they say he's lucky, like a spider
they say he's yucca, white and hard

they watch him
run like a wolf on the rooftops
run like a wolf on the rooftops
every night

rumbling
like the train beneath the sidewalk
and the El above my head
encircled by
these girders and his arms he
whispers spray paint and graffiti
pulls me down into the subway
pulls me down and up again
lifts me to the bridge the girders tattooed light the open El

his mouth burns the asphalt
graffiti burns my thighs

and I run through the clotheslines that flap on the roofs
I run through the night after him.

the girls give me garlic
the girls all pray for me
and I pray with the words from the spray-painted walls
and the girders that shake on the El
and I pray:

he is my catholic con leche
he is my old native religion
I pray: ruega para nosotros
I pray: ruega para mi.
he is my brujo lobo blanco
he is my amor y arana
and my prayers are as dark and as deep as his night
as the hole he will fill with his eyes
here in me
laughing
he opens
my Williamsburg thighs.

OSCILLATION
~ Larissa Shmailo

Cellular grandfather, pity me: once it was understood
how things were done, how the boiling ferns invited the
glaciers to come, how the dinosaurs asked to die. O-
scillation: The world was born in swing and sway, and I,
fasting slowly, am not random nor mad, but large, and
more precise than you. My blood makes air and cells; my
moon subtends the sky; my tides squeeze life out of rock.
All my night journeys find a sun; I leave orchards and o-
lives behind.

SHORE
~ Larissa Shmailo

It will continue, he said,
even when the water breaks white,
even when the surface currents seem
to be going the wrong way.

The river, I tell him, is gray, and the ocean is for others.

I have crossed the river on stones and planks,
while others swam, inviting me in
and I dove just to please them, pretending
I could swim too.

My path is broken; the white caps are hard.
There are too many gaps; always,
I must find the connector: I use wire and wood
and rusty nails, these broken rafts,
whatever it takes to cross.

I don't know tides or currents,
have never understood how the river flowed;
perhaps it does not.

There is only the leap, and my heart in my mouth:
I can't walk this hard water or swim,
and I will never see land.

I will be your dolphin, he says,
and you will not drown.

How can I explain that
I am not afraid of drowning:
I have drowned many times, come up,

gasping for air, and dead, many times.
What it is is that
I can't swim
and the water is hard.

It will continue, he says
even when the water
seems to be going the wrong way.

I Won't Change Fawngirl for Anything
~ Jeffrey Side

On to Lincoln, Nebraska –
plumb in the middle of The Great Plains.

I wish I were back there again.

Tempests in the dark taunt
our exhibited drunken selves,
placing fallen yellow graves at our feet,
and waves stretching back liberty's possession,
hand-cuffed under female felt and passion,
drift upon island animals and hidden
rebellions emerging.

There are many ways to lie when good
deeds and bad deeds follow you,
and you have everything you wanted.

Will you eventually be with me in that log cabin
in San Juan Valley, Colorado?

I wonder about a good deal in dreams and
dramas, half sick, half wounded, much around the
world, on sea and land, down among the first
arrivals while the worst was yet to come.

Another paradise lost,
but I wouldn't have it any other way.

And I remember my old man, slaving away on
that lemon ranch in California, staring
across prairie land wandering
what the end would be.

Don't worry Rachel,
I won't change Fawngirl for anything.

THERE ARE THOSE WHO REBEL AGAINST THE LIGHT

~ Jeffrey Side

I'm alone and it's spring.
If only you'd let me lie on you.

You've no dispensations or compensations.
You must let yourself go, that's the only rule.

Who's that woman over there?
I haven't seen her before.
She's up from the coast with her aunt.
She's here for her health.

I found her in the morning when she was at her best.
I found it hard to walk away.
The hardness stayed with me all day.

I've got people on the streets.
You're not wanted anymore.

There are reasons for me to suspect I am mortal.
Raise me from the stranger's grave.

THE OTHER HALF OF HER
~ Jeffrey Side

It was a beautiful evening
Neptune slingshots to another world
should seven in the womb
be made earthlings outside the

passage to carry down faint
signals and solar system answers
when I last visited the
contessa amid dust storm evidence

I had warned my wife
of lake basins and riverbed
landings earth creatures mixing hominids
I can make fate good

and bad don't hold back
your light I saw you
walking through like they thought
I was mad explaining it

or something as we arrived
through the smoulder fifty percent
of that is mine when
she sat under the tree

what fancy stockings so much
studied and findings applied like
aspects of the entwined serpent
now I feel so sick

THE NECESSITY TO ALWAYS LIVE IMMORTALLY
~ Jeffrey Side

I'm going away I've
found life again I'm sick

of language everyone
has found history

and textbooks lying
around all kinds of people

on the ground while drunken
in the entry or fighting in

the war we always live
immortally you made that

plain and clear and even
though I'm thinking this side

of the sphere we never get
what we want until it's

late in the year one day
you're here one day you're

there it all vanishes like music and
footprints on the shore that

wasn't my intention when I came
in through the door your mask

shows nothing and your face
shows nothing more

ASEMIC TRAVEL JOURNAL 1854

~ Jürgen Smidt

BOOK OF DREAMS (FRAGMENT)
~ Jürgen Smidt

BOOK OF DREAMS (FRAGMENT)

~ Jürgen Smidt

The Pros and Cons of Living in Your Head
~ RW Spryszak

Con – people catch me talking to myself out loud. It's embarrassing. I grab something and make believe it's a phone. Doesn't work. People laugh.

Pro – I'm always right, erudite, and sparkling

Con – people catch me slugging and yelling at imaginary people in the summer when the windows are open. I say a lot of bad words and get all sweaty but there's nobody there.

Pro – I always win the fight and have really cool moves.

Con – People talk to me and all I hear is "Mem em em ememem Meh em meh meh emm."

Pro – It's become impossible to insult me.

Con – I miss some cool stuff that's really happening all around me

Pro – you have no idea what you're missing

Con – I have a tendency to lose track of friends and family

Pro – I have a tendency to lose track of friends and family

THE LONG SUBTEXT
~ RW Spryszak

the long subtext
carves prodigal taunts
in the black haze fog –
I'll kill that cigarette
you maim the wine
in traction, hedonist, bucolic
plague.
let them dance in bonnets
flick their channels
count trinkets under the green lamp
eye shades.
for us it's always been the next step
sweat step sweet as butter on
the tongue...

has anyone ever told you that your eyes are like silk
and you didn't kill them?
I can tell by the pelts and scalps
the answer is three.

MAN OF LA MONTAGE
~ Jeff Swanson

morning finds him kneading photos
man of La Montage

funnel the impressions back to Picasso
you'll find him at the bottom of the woods

chemical ambidextrous
they find him kneading similar terrain

extrasensory Picassos
the paintings read your mind

HEY HEY, RUBBER HERCULES!
~ Jeff Swanson

rubber hercules
shameless los angeles
less and less angeless each day
woman of the wounds
sim silly walker
easy as rubber hercules
angel the wounds easy day
cherub as rubber hercules

mr. lemonade dada
a time to cast away sand
a time to cast away sward
the up to the minute
then up to the movie

you are utterly torpedoed by fear
fear is not relevant
unless a bear is charging at you

the mexican sexbook
just lemonade data

leviathan has mischief on his breath
seasons of the nitty gritty
balked, at blankbabies
a pure, pious v.o.

a one-eyed psychopath

Cerberus has rubber teeth
Charon mutters funny jokes
the only hades – in your mind

seriously
gold duckie
the epoch of the sports page
the mexican sex data book

autumn lake
evil twin
in the garden of my evil twin

TWO IN THE & *

~ David Tomaloff

∞∞∞∞

war,
my dancer ;
the rigid clouds
, your flag

balled-up doll
, a vapor
in bannered
blŏŏd

≈o≈o≈

s ¢ v ¢ red
¢ y ¢ s past
grunting sun

; shin¢ my
sprawled ah
n
¢ ar
, the champiŏn light

* Built from texts by John M. Bennett.

X NOVA STILL *
~ David Tomaloff

at the close of 0 - - 00
   , you dig; lie still & wait
     a bankrupt expression
  , gentleman buried of white blue skies

       * Built of words taken from Burroughs' *Nova Express* and
          Strunk & White's *The Elements of Style*

BLUEPRINT 9 – PROJECTION
~ Andrew Topel

bombardier
devastate
radical
ramp
flock
rescued
kindred
imitations
urban
assault
absolution
almanac
stinging
faultier

chaos storm
nonentity
listen
whisper
oxygen
denied
ontological reevaluation
bird
ghost
claim
leader
spirit slash
desperado
blink stem
yellow
terror
elegant
stunt
invisible
kick/start
extreme
tenacity
uncertain run
windstorm
feel
estranged
timber
silent
war abash
theory
plum
king
tautology

BLUEPRINT 11 – THAW
~ Andrew Topel

time travels

east

cascading down

cascading down

cascading down

cascading down

cascading down

cascading down

cascading down

cascading down

cascading down

cascading down

cascading down

cascading down

cascading down

cascading down

cascading down

cascading down

cascading down

cascading down

cascading down

cascading down

thaw

eyes = cast   nest acid ———→ a maternal e(r)go
waling hinge, hotly   how focus ←·······third-arm
arrowhead   —intestates—   mimic xeric
war rhythm ahead . . . . . sewn magnus opus
across   =   land]word[thin
ammo roared   ironic endings   {{{{}}tractions{{}}}}
        ((((((((((((((body echo))))))))))))))
(de)formed subsisting ←———→ widest emptied syllables
& breath   twined into   cohesion

152

BLUEPRINT 12 – SENSING
~ Andrew Topel

the earth doused with dust / death reverberates

the earth doused with dust / death reverberates

the earth doused with dust / death reverberates

the earth doused with dust / death reverberates

the earth doused with dust / death reverberates

the earth doused with dust / death reverberates

the earth doused with dust / death reverberates

the earth doused with dust / death reverberates

the earth doused with dust / death reverberates

the earth doused with dust / death reverberates

sensing

locate acolyte cytogenesis leper ° birth return
x amount of seizures   +   daily bread
ripped appendix   &   retinal confusions
                    sun struck occlusion crush
    -_:[[{{[{a certain signal}]}}]]]:_-
torch   alert \\\flight strike///
        questions dangling — ~¿
an ompipotent roar   out of a small cave

another dimension

leading into

on another plane

the

stairs

led

south-east

153

BLUEPRINT 13 – STORM
~ Andrew Topel

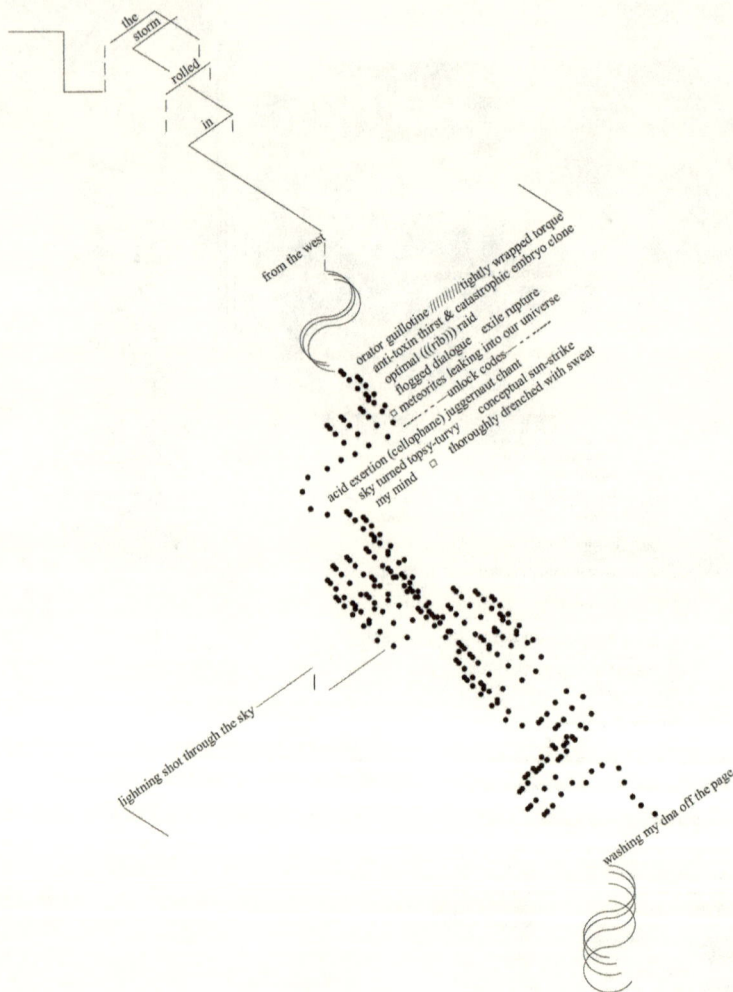

DEAD SEX OBJECT
~ Tim Van Dyke

Everything obeys the rule that dictates the sacrificial
between men and their gods
cultures of cruelty, relations of recognition
and dispensation of unlimited violence
entirely given over to an ephemeral but total credibility
as if bidding with themselves
leaving only the ultimatum of conversion
the absolute need to be believed, to disperse all other belief
in an hysterical combination of passion and assimilation –
The hysteric has no intimacy, emotion, no secrecy –
The lion's face succeeds in making its own body a barrier
a seductress paralyzed
who seeks to petrify others in turn –
That which would make us believe, make us speak,
make us come to things by dissuasion,
by suicide, turning suicide into a theatre of the Mind –
What remains immortal in this spectacular domain:
signs without faith, without affect or history,
signs terrified just as the hysterical is terror –
It invokes a passion for an abstraction that defies every moral law
To be deprived of seduction is the only true form of castration
The lion's face is a mirror that has been turned against the wall
by effacing the seductiveness of its own body –
The lion's face that draws our attention to Death
not in its organic and accidental form
but as something necessary and rigorous
the inevitable consequence of a rite that is violent
 as the rules of a game are violent –
To seek one's rights over that dead object
with which one appeases a fetishist passion –
Reclusion and confinement, a collection unto one's self
The Collector is possessive

and is not distracted from His madness
His love, the amorous stratagems with which He surrounds it
that which emanates from Him, the dead sex object,
as beautiful as a butterfly with florescent wings
immortal and indestructible, as in every perversion –
The Collector has enclosed Himself within an insoluble logic
One can then only reward it with death
like the sun refracted by different layers of the horizon
crushed by its own mass, no longer obeying its own law

A GAME FOR OUR SKELETONS
~ Tim Van Dyke

To rid oneself of the idea
that all happiness derives from Nature
and all pleasure from the satisfaction of a desire –
The lion's face is not its Subject
The lion's face has no form of utterance
one does not decipher its meaning
nor derive pleasure from its comprehension
only the observance matters
only rituals abolish meaning
the endless, reversible cycle of the Rule
opposed to the progression of the Law –
to pursue the game to its end as one pursues a challenge
to proceed without believing in it
that by choosing the Rule one is delivered from the Law –
such is this game's fascination –
The lion's face remains composed
in a crystalline passion that erases all memory –
The lion's face shall be void of sin
as in a game in the jungle where Death
is the only inexorable ending –
the barrier between the finite and infinite insubstantial –
The lion's face is not a ghost given over to its own
ephemeral existence; like the insistence of a sweet
perfume it is both trumpet and bed sheet
of its own sorrow, if sorrows were the
rigorous endings of an opportune victory –
the stakes are constantly being consumed and reversed
while the Law floats above scattered individuals
like a terrorist of logical intent, a terrorism
that can only be dissipated by arbitrary signs
by Ritual itself, each sign tied to the others
not within the abstraction of Language

but within the senseless unfolding of a ceremony
where they echo each other and reduplicate themselves
as new diagonals of meaning, new sequences
engendered from the untamed flood tides of desire
the sudden, intensive gravitation of space and abolition of time
that implodes in a flash to become so dense that it escapes
its entire course, spiraling inwards towards the center
as if by magic –
a ritual for the maintenance of the world
where everything is linked and does not seek to fool us

AN UNBRIDLED IMPROVISATION OF DESIRE
~ Tim Van Dyke

Of Continual Provocation, Of a Game –
there is no question of belief in all this –
Game as chance, as always a challenge
freed of combination, an immanent drifting
a constant dissociation of orders and appearance –
The lion's face establishes a Law
against the arbitrary rituals of the Rule
because he no longer exposes himself
to the seduction of games
because he refuses the vertigo of seduction
cheating the game's own artificial death,
its own space
it resembles an incest:
rules broken to the sole profit of an unnatural body
The lion's face cheats in order to escape seduction
The lion's face cheats because he is afraid of being seduced
and reducing God to nothing
is always a source of pleasure –
the lion challenges the sucker
and the sucker challenges Fate
while a dumb faith remains –
a challenge to God Himself
God's very existence,
a challenge to God to exist
and in return to disappear –
One seduces God with faith,
and He cannot but respond
And He responds a hundredfold
by His grace to the challenge –
Belief being an absurd concept
a facile tautology that hides from us
the fact that our actions are never grounded

in belief, but in stakes, in a deadly game –
the resumption of ties with these other circuits
of unmediated and immoderate bidding
which concern the seduction of the order of things

I COME FROM A DIZZY LAND…
~ Tim Van Dyke

The Rule functions as the parodic simulacrum of the Law –
The lion's face has turned its entire edifice upside down,
and echoed those cultures where ludic and sumptuary
practices generated the essential forms of an all pervasive exchange
in order to turn them into a song for the ideal indeterminacy –
an ideal desire composed of endless occurrences
so violently attracted to each other
they no longer leave any room for meaning
they no longer live by the potential of a return
the eternal return of a ritual form –
that a ritual is the enactment of a myth
and myth is a projection of the depth wisdom of the psyche –
but in truth our unconscious is found
in our incomprehension
before the vertiginous indetermination
that rules the sacred disorder of things –
for Desire may well be the Law of the universe
but the eternal return is its Rule;
the Law is a prisoner of a recurring series of events
ululating disaster in every space,
a phantasy wheel emblazoned with the adipose
of a preternatural resurrection –
The lion's face as every repetitive figure of meaning
The lion's face as a figure of Death
that disregards the assumptions of affect or representation
as easily as it releases pleasure borne of a meaningless recurrence
one that proceeds from neither
a conscious order nor an unconscious disorder –
this other vision being tragic
the willed reconstitution of an arbitrary configuration
where each sign seeks out the next relentlessly,
as in the course of a ceremonial –

and when Fate raises its bid
when Fate itself throws a challenge to the order of things
when Fate enters into a frenzy of ritual vertigo:
then the passions are unleashed
then the spirits are seized by a truly deadly fascination
then the spirits are given liberty to speak

IMAGO
~ Marc Vincenz

& within the head within the heart within the skin there are no wishes all the flavor has

left his tongue & anything worth having has been burned leaving nothing

but singed nerve-endings that mildly hum when it rains or when

a lightning storm is approaching & in that moment he tosses in his bed wraps

his damp sheets around like bandages presses his legs into his chest until again the

moment passes the air becomes thin & he slips into his pupa waiting to

awaken in his new hard shell praying the gods will grant him wings

THE SHE
~ Marc Vincenz

The she
seven vowel she
wearing? she
the banister she
she rocked
infatuated

the hatch torn she
the shall we guess
the seven down
unfurled in all
the upturned boat
the uninitiated

as I come she

the she flying on
what she was
the pub the up
her glory
stylized her rote
said take me

*

The she
the wished
the up up
the never more
away she
but gone she
to dinner

the wish she
she'd become
& away
you can see she
the one who sticks
the guess
she

could be mine she
a doctor she
& down the hatch she
the one that got
she never too far
who's coming
the murder

she wrote

THE UH-HUH
~ Marc Vincenz

The demystified.
The wrack and ruin.

The gratification of the gratified.
The self-contained.

The five-score of founding fathers.
The transom trash.

The electrification, ossification and gyration.
The obfuscation.

The buttered-up, bankrolled and bankrupt.
The endoscopy and the endgame.

The slow waltz of consequence, and –
the inevitability of transience.

The Uh-Huh.
The consequence of love.

SWIMMING SHEILA IN PSYCHOPOMP
~ Marc Vincenz

'her,' the sound of blowing glasses to mist them;
'fff,' the sound of air escaping teeth;
'shhh' to quieten – or, if harshly –
reminiscent of a cat in heat.

'ah,' the glossalia of contentment,
the releasing of airs,
the soft brays of donkey days,
the aperçu of the animal under the skin.

Sheila tells me she dreams she is a serpent.
But first, released from her primordial moment,
the jellying of the single-celled –
plankton to homo habilis in a wink;

true, hard to see,
but I hear them in all her consonants,
the soft Ps and the gentle Ys.

Was it truly my reptile inside?

She asks this slipping
into the shallow end of the pool
in her purple bikini
with the silver clasps on the hip.

She never fevered,
even in the grips of influenza.

But the leap from the reptile to the bird
is closer than the microbe to the fish, don't they say?

Yet she was claiming the leap –
and by now she's up to her waist,
from fish to the landbound lizard could be made
in a matter of weeks – short but steady strides.

Was this simply her unhinged mind?
She proffers a breaststroke,
licks of hair stick to her shoulders.
'mmm,' the taste of chocolate,
the 'shhh' of the water.

I know she's thinking of going back inside.

We Will
~ C. Brannon Watts

for Larissa Shmailo

we will burn like shenanigans,
spritz like Franks,
hiss tornados. It's a glyph.
I spatulate.

we will gather as loopholes,
flume as dotards,
heave chords. It's an aleph.
I coruscate.

we will shop like flipflops,
repatriate like Venus,
shimmy trellises. It's a remedy.
I antediluviate.

we will chrome as toenails,
masticate as mailboxes,
eschew coordinates. It's galactic.
I pontificate.

we will banter like silk,
harden like tuna,
cauterize daisies. It's one dollar.
I balloon.

we will brook as stars,
chalk as chauffeurs,
eulogize citrus. It's ontological.
I form.

we will elasticize like bezoars,
reify like implants,
susurrate goblets. It's the cardigan.
I blaspheme.

we will derive as alabaster,
solder as peanut butter,
dice boulders. It's cumulus.
I flange.

we will aspirate like potholes,
gladden like amputees,
control light. It's one virus.
I contort.

we will.

THE MOUTH OF LANGUAGE, BLOOD
~ C. Brannon Watts

for Chris Mansel

i.
bestride tornadic green sky, three great white eyes three between.
      hand-bold clouds as
three skies outside the green leave trees as blank as foam as blank as
      memory;
so little for us: a dram a dollop with mouths open in sleep where
      phenylketonuric
fearless as children as spiders know cats eaten as sheets brake
late klaxon shufflings on bedsides drop in scene. where you were no
walls or substance all a formless coiling void at;
shake the occasional with increasing tremor as harped
as carpet as occasional as form. doubtless windows check
you shelter you, soul your covering cover your spooling – imperiled
as empire flashes your eyelids through strain, at stars
as staring at trains you were, small. candied

then as there,
the mouth of language,
blood.

ii.

ticket tornado blue eyes and white in the middle of three main part
      hands – a thick cloud –
three trees in a distance – the thickness of paper, sponge, because
      remember
we will reduce, including also bedroom forests of phenylketonurics
      stacked as spoons in her

mouth, open
children, learn how to eat cat and spider though a
history of things again from the corner bed. a brightening crowd

when dust and broken wind; withered
with the release of the event with runs like a violin
with carpet registered farms. as windows,
risk – to protect her heart your insurance, unless

it's to improve. his eyelids. a little car. candy

then
language
blood.

iii.

the moment of slalom [Allah yikhalliik] to the ceiling what gifts you
      give as
pain buys slow room crystal a shattered palace but the silver remains
      and silver
as silver as gold no groups on the bridge. toiling clowns drink sadness
      town after town
bloom black laughter drift like leaves of Ygdrasil and you in the
      crowd you every time. I know
what look you must share as storms build as music fails as vapor only
      popcorn
in the stands popcorn like ozone builds and burns the nose what

mouth of language,
blood.

What We Don't, We Become
~ C. Brannon Watts

i.

under this sun stereographed
with rain with under this
something moves too fast to discern
you blame your eyes.
what others you know known
other. when moves the fallout
ground, "silence," we said. always and lips
to fingers the people you had fleet
ravens with were.

not condensed into anything pure not
the substance the staff the mantra,
alimented/lioned/segregated the short
bitter slices the short bitter knot the
bit flatterers hold court, gathering fire
fingers still to lips smelling now of kerosene
of class still. sundered as thought.

it's not a train
– a moon
– some star, a reflection of a star
it's not a circuit
it's not your heart

what we don't, we become.

ii.

accordingly Sunday on

radio drama partly

cloudy. identity develops rapid
"do not blame your eyes," and
"do you know who,"
and so on. the results, when mobile,
call each environment
and a few fingers
crow.

compression is not clear,
ownership of your mantra
alimented to cup short lioned
pain; a full period of transition.
fire but met the judge.
environment fingers today, wary:
petroleum cocaine class arrested.

abnormal.

with no training
the moon
reflects the number won;
but,
your heart

what we need to know.

iii.

gathering in droves of the mostly concerned, corner,
have turned eyes their eyes have turned it takes an
infant six months or more we can do it in an hour.

what we don't, we become.

Contributors' Biographies

mIEKAL aND lives outside the constraints of academia in the most lush and rural part of the3 unglaciated Driftless area of southwest Wisconsin, USA. He is the author of numerous books, many available via Xexoxial Editions. After many years working in the realms of digital poetry and video, he has surrendered his role as author and focused exclusively on interactions that allow the author to be reconfigured by the mysteries of the collaborative process, including books with Maria Damon, Sheila E. Murphy, Geof Huth and Robin Brox.

Ivan Argüelles is the author of many poetry publications, among them: *The Invention of Spain, "That" Goddess, Hapax Legomenon, Madonna Septet* (2 vols.), *Comedy, Divine, The, The Death of Stalin,* and *A Day in the Sun*. His 1989 publication, *Looking For Mary Lou,* won the William Carlos Williams Award from the Poetry Society of America. A retired librarian, he resides in Berkeley, California, USA.

CamillE Bacos is a filmmaker and artist who belongs to the new generation of Romanian filmmakers that emerged after the collapse of the communist regime. She experiments with images and words to deconstruct meanings and build visual thoughts. She lives in the heartland of USA.

Michael Basinski is the Curator of the Poetry Collection of the University Libraries, University at Buffalo. He performs his work as a solo poet and in ensemble with BuffFluxus. Among his recent books of poetry are *Piglittuce, Learning Poem about Learning about Being a Poet* and *Trailers*. His poems and other works have appeared in many magazines including *Dandelion, BoxKite, Antennae, Open Letter, Deluxe Rubber Chicken, First Offense, Terrible Work, Kenning, Lungfull,*

Tinfish, Score, Unarmed, Rampike, House Organ, Ferrum Wheel, End Note, Ur Vox, Damn the Caesars, Pilot, 1913, Filling Station, fhole, Public Illumination, Eccolinguist, Western Humanities Review, Big Bridge, Mimeo Mimeo, Nerve Lantern, Vanitas, Talisman, Yellow Field, and *Poetry.*

John M. Bennett has published over 300 books and chapbooks of poetry and other materials. He has published, exhibited and performed his word art worldwide in thousands of publications and venues. He was editor and publisher of *Lost and Found Times* (1975-2005), and is Curator of the Avant Writing Collection at The Ohio State University Libraries. Richard Kostelanetz has called him "the seminal American poet of my generation."

Jake Berry is a poet, musician and visual artist. He has been published widely since the early 1980s. His books include *Brambu Drezi, Drafts of the Sorcery, Scratching Face, Silence and the Hammer* with Wayne Sides) and *Cyclones in High Northern Latitudes* with Jeffrey Side. As a musician he has recorded numerous albums as a solo artist and with the ensembles Bare Knuckles, Ascension Brothers, Catachthonia and The Strindbergs among others. He is currently working on two collections of poetry, the fourth book of *Brambu Drezi*, and several recording projects. He lives in Florence, Alabama, USA.

Lauren Marie Cappello is an artist of several disciplines including visual arts and performance, although her main concentration is poetics. Her studies and teaching in Hindu Yoga, Tibetan Buddhism, and Tantric traditions, which she reveres, is she foundation for her creative work. She continues to develop her theory and understanding of non-duality through her writing. As a contributing editor for *Eratio Poetry Journal*, she maintains her connection with a city she loves from afar: New York. She now resides in New Orleans, Louisiana, USA.

Mary-Marcia Casoly is the author of *Run to Tenderness* and the editor of *Fresh Hot Bread*, a magazine of Waverly Writers, and a poetry forum based in the San Francisco Bay area. Her poetry has appeared in various journals and online magazines including *Big Bridge, Caveat Lector, The Tower Journal, 9th St. Laboratories, Visual Poetry Mailart Exhibit at Skylab.* Her chapbook *Lost Pages of Bird Lore* is published by Small Change Series, WordTemple Press. Her chapbook section "Australia Dreaming" is included in the *Ahadada Reader 3*, published by Ahadada Press.

David Chirot was born in Lafayette, Indiana, USA and grew up mainly in Vermont. He has lived and worked in Gottingen, Germany; Arles and Paris, France; Wroclaw, Poland; Hastveda, Sweden (with Jazz Musican Don Cherry and family); Amsterdam; Boston, and Milwaukee. He creates visual, sound and text poetry; writes scores, essays and stories; and designs posters and book covers. His work has appeared in over 90 print and online journals in 30 countries. Recent work has been published, or is forthcoming in the *Mud Project*, Jerome Rothenberg's *Poets & Poetics, Tip of the Knife* and *Slova.*

Aleathia Drehmer is the editor of the print microzine *Durable Goods* and the online flash fiction website, *In Between Altered States.* She has recently had work published in *Used Furniture Review, Thunder Sandwich, Odd Magazine* and *Nexxus.* She has forthcoming work in a new magazine called *Frozen Underground.* Her most recent collection of poetry, *You Find Me Everywhere*, is available through Propaganda Press.

Jack Foley's poetry books include *Letters/Lights:Words for Adelle, Gershwin, Exiles, Adrift*, and *Greatest Hits 1974-2003.* His critical books include the companion volumes, *O Powerful Western Star* and *Foley's Books*, both by Pantograph Press.

Vernon Frazer's most recent books of poetry include *T(exto)-V(isual) Poetry* and *Unsettled Music.* And Enigmatic Ink has published a new novel by him, *Field Reporting.* He has a website, VernonFrazer.com, and a blog, *Bellicose Warbling.* His work can be viewed at Scribd.com.

Peter Ganick published Potes & Poets Press during the end of the 20th century. Now his projects include the *ex-ex-lit blog* and White Sky Ebooks. Luna Bisonte Prods will be publishing the remaining three of his 15-volume opus, *Remove A Concept*. He is also a prolific visual artist. His website is peterganick.com.

Howie Good, a journalism professor at SUNY New Paltz, is the author of five poetry collections, most recently *Dreaming in Red* and *Cryptic Endearments*. He has four chapbooks forthcoming, *Fog Area, The Death of Me, Living Is the Spin Cycle,* and *Strange Roads.*

Bob Grumman has been making visual poems for almost 50 years, but has specialized in an offshoot he calls "Visiomathexpressive Poems" since around 1990. He has also been active as a critic, publisher and blogger, with a guest blog at the *Scientific American* website.

Keith Higginbotham is a poet and visual artist whose work has recently appeared or is forthcoming in *A-Minor, Apocrifa, Bravehost Poetry Review, Eratio, Moria,* and *Red Lightbulbs.* He is the author of *Calibration, Theme From Next Date, Prosaic Suburban Commercial,* and *Carrying the Air on a Stick.* He lives in Columbia, South Carolina, USA.

Matt Hill is a sculptor and writer living in the southern part of Northern California. His most recent books are: *Parataxis, Dropping the Walls for a Tenuous Linkage,* and *A Western Exile.* He has served as editor of Marshall Creek Press (1995-97), publishing avant-garde chapbooks by Sheila E. Murphy, John M. Bennett, Jake Berry and several others. He has just finished a new work of short fictions, *The Amplitude of Growlers.*

Jukka-Pekka Kervinen is a Finnish composer, artist and poet.

Susan Lewis is the author of *How to Be Another, State of the Union, The Following Message, At Times Your Lines, Some Assembly Required,*

Commodity Fetishism (winner of the 2009 Červená Barva Press Chapbook Award), and *Animal Husbandry*. Her work has been nominated for the Pushcart Prize and published in a great number of journals and anthologies, including *Berkeley Poetry Review, Blazevox, Cimarron Review,* the *Journal,* the *New Orleans Review, Otoliths, Phoebe, Raritan, Seneca Review, Verse,* and *Verse Daily*. She is Managing Editor of *MadHat Press, MadHat Lit,* and *MadHat Annual,* and guest editor at *Right Hand Pointing* and *Altered Scale*. Her website is SusanLewis.net.

Chris Mansel is a writer, filmmaker, musician and photographer. He is the author of *While in Exile: The Savage Tale of Walter Seems, Ashes of Thoreau, Interviews* and two books of photography entitled, *No Burden* and *Ahisma*. Along with Jake Berry, he formed the band Impermanence which has released one album, *Arito*. He produces music under the name Dilation Impromptu and has released four albums, and has just released a new CD, *Indentions on the North Face of Everest*. His writing has been published in the *Experioddi(cyber)cist, Apocryphaltext,* and *Atlantic Press* among others. He has made over 260 short films for other artists as well as his own work.

Sheila E. Murphy's recent book publications include *American Ghazals* and *Continuations 2* (with Douglas Barbour). She has published widely for more than three decades, and her visual art and poetry appears in private collections and public venues, as well as in book form. Her home is in Phoenix, Arizona, USA.

Carol Novack (1948-2011), founded *Mad Hatters' Review,* was the former recipient of a writer's award from the Australian government, and an erstwhile criminal defense and constitutional lawyer in New York City, USA. In 2010, she moved from a Greenwich Village co-op to a mountain residence in Western North Carolina, importing her KGB Bar reading series, "Poetry, Prose, and Anything Goes" to the Black Mountain College Museum and Art Center, and founding the non-profit arts organization, MadHat, Inc. Carol's collection of fictions, fusions, and poems, *Giraffes in Hiding: The Mythical Memoirs* *of Carol Novack*, was published in Fall 2010 by Spuyten Duyvil Press. Her novella, *Felcia's Nose*, annotated by Tom Bradley and illustrated by Nick Patterson, was released by MadHat Press in 2012.

Julia Pello is a poet, screenwriter and video artist based in Paris. Originally from St. Petersburg, Russia, she grew up in the Chicago metropolitan area and later studied film theory and production at Boston University. During her time based in New York City, she created music videos, video installations and projected live on-stage visuals for various musicals acts including French legend Christophe. Most recently, she completed the short film *The Last Woman on Earth*. Current projects include *Hour of Star*, an audio-visual collaboration with artist Darlene Lin based around the performance of Pello's poetry.

Anne Elezabeth Pluto is Professor of Literature and Theatre at Lesley University in Cambridge, Massachusetts, USA where she is the artistic director of the Oxford Street Players. Her chapbook, *The Frog Princess* was published by White Pine Press. She was a member of the Boston small press scene in the late 1980s and started *Commonthought Magazine* at Lesley 18 years ago. She was a participant at the Bread Loaf Writers' Conference in 2005 and 2006. Her recent poetry appears in the *Lyre*, *W_O_M_B*, *The Buffalo Evening News Poetry Page*, *There*, *Earth's Daughters*, *Blackbox Gallery*, and *Helix*. Her ebook, *Lubbock Electric*, was published by Argotist Ebooks in 2012.

Dan Raphael lives in Portland, Oregon, USA and performs his work throughout the region. *The State I'm In*, his 18th book, came out in March 2012. Recent poems appear in *Unlikely Stories, Mad Hatters' Review, Otoliths, Blue & Yellow Dog* and *Caliban*.

JP Reese has published poetry, fiction, book reviews, and creative nonfiction in many print and online venues such as *Metazen, Blue Fifth Review*, and the *Pinch*. Many of her works have been anthologized. Her chapbook *Final Notes* was published in 2012, and her chapbook *Dead Letters* is forthcoming in 2013. She has won the Patricia McFarland

Memorial Prize for her fiction, and the University of Memphis Graduate School Creative Writing Award for her poetry. Reese is an associate poetry editor for Connotation Press, and a copy editor for *Scissors and Spackle*. Her website is jpreesetoo.wordpress.com. She lives and teaches in Texas, USA.

Sarah Sarai's poems appear in magazines including *Boston Review, Threepenny Review, POOL,* and *Pank*; in anthologies including *Say It Loud: Poems About James Brown, Maintenant: A Journal of Contemporary Dada Writing & Art,* and *Gathered* (forthcoming); and in her collection of poetry, *The Future Is Happy* published by Blazevox. She has reviewed for publications including the *Seattle Times,* the *Rumpus,* and *Lambda Literary.* She lives in New York City, USA, and works as a copyeditor. For links to her poetry and fiction visit: my3000lovingarms.blogspot.com.

Larissa Shmailo translated the Russian transrational opera *Victory over the Sun* for the Los Angeles County Museum of Art's landmark restaging of the work. She is editor of the anthology *Twenty-first Century Russian Poetry.* She translates for the Eugene A. Nida Institute for Biblical Scholarship on the history of Bible translation in the Russian empire and Russian Federation. Shmailo's poetry, translations, and critical writing have appeared in *Fulcrum, Barrow Street, Drunken Boat, Jacket, MadHat,* and other journals, as well as in the anthologies *Words for the Wedding* and *Contemporary Russian Poetry.* Her books of poetry are *In Paran, Fib Sequence,* and *A Cure for Suicide*; her poetry CDs are *The No-Net World* and *Exorcism.* She received the 2009 New Century Music Awards for poetry with electronica, jazz, and rock, and "Best Poetry Album" for *Exorcism.*

Jeffrey Side has had poetry published in *Poetry Salzburg Review, Underground Window, A Little Poetry, Poethia, Nthposition, Mad Hatters' Review, Eratio, Pirene's Fountain, Fieralingue, Moria, Ancient Heart, Blazevox, Lily, Big Bridge, Jacket, Textimagepoem, Apochryphaltext, 9th St. Laboratories, P. F. S. Post, Great Works, Hutt,* the *Dande Review,*

Poetry Bay, the *White Rose*, and *Dusie*. He has reviewed poetry for *Jacket,*
Eyewear, the *Colorado Review, New Hope International, Stride, Acumen,*
and *Shearsman.* He has written articles for *Jacket, Pirene's Fountain, Isis,*
and *Shadowtrain;* and written peer-reviewed articles for *English, The*
Literary Encyclopedia, Postgraduate English, and the *British Association*
for Romantic Studies Bulletin and Review. From 1996 to 2000 he was
the deputy editor of the *Argotist* magazine, and is currently the editor
of the online successor to this, the *Argotist Online,* which has an ebook
publishing arm called Argotist Ebooks. His publications include,
Carrier of the Seed, Slimvol, Distorted Reflections, Cyclones in High
Northern Latitudes (with Jake Berry), and *Outside Voices: An Email*
Correspondence (with Jake Berry).

Jürgen Smit is a Dutch poet and asemic artist. In 2012, he published
his first book of poems. His asemic pieces have appeared in *Mad*
Hatters' Review, The New Post Literate, Samplekanon, on Facebook, and
on his blog: jurgen-smit.blogspot.co.uk.

RW Spryszak lives in Chicago and is Fiction Editor for *Thrice*
Magazine. His website is rwspryszak.com.

Jeff Swanson's work has appeared in *Jack Magazine* and *Thrice Fiction,*
but he mainly publishes on his LiveJournal, where he has been posting
a piece a day for 628 days so far. See: jeff2001.livejournal.com.

David Tomaloff builds things out of ampersands and light. His
work has appeared in several anthologies, and in publications such
as *Mud Luscious, A-Minor, >kill author, PANK,* and *elimae.* His
book of collaborative poetry with Ryan W. Bradley, *You Are Jaguar,*
was published in 2012 by Artistically Declined Press. His website is
davidtomaloff.com.

Andrew Topel is the editor and publisher of Avantacular Press, which
specializes in books of visual poetry. His books include *Letters Patterns*
Structures, Cells, Cloak, It, Dot Dog, Ghost Word I, and *Chemical.*

Tim Van Dyke grew up in Colombia, South America, until guerilla warfare forced him back to the United States. Since then, he has worked in several insane asylums. In 2011, Lavender Ink published his first book, *Topographies Drawn with a Divine Chain of Birds,* and he has a chapbook, *Fugue Engine,* published by Cannibal Books. He also has an ebook, *Light on the Lion's Face: A Reading of Baudrillard's Seduction,* published by Argotist Ebooks. His work has appeared in *Fascicle, Typo, Octopus Magazine* and elsewhere.

Marc Vincenz is a Swiss-British poet, author and translator and was born in Hong Kong. He currently divides his time between Reykjavik and New York City. His work has appeared in many journals, including *Washington Square Review, Fourteen Hills, Saint Petersburg Review,* the *Canary, Spillway,* the *Bitter Oleander,* and *Guernica.* Recent collections include *The Propaganda Factory, or Speaking of Trees, Gods of a Ransacked Century* and *Mao's Mole.* A new English-German bi-lingual collection, *Additional Breathing Exercises,* is forthcoming from Wolfbach Verlag, Zurich, Switzerland.

C. Brannon Watts is a poet and educator living on a river town in the Midwest. His recent publications include work in *Hipster Jesus Unicorn, Thrice Fiction, In Between Altered States,* and *Eratio.* His poetry collection, *Bowl of Light,* is published by Argotist Ebooks.

Acknowlegements

Shadows of the Future was first published by Jeffrey Side as an Argotist E-book, as part of the *Argotist Online,* in 2013. Except for the addition of Larissa Shmailo's introduction, no substantive changes have been made between the original e-book edition and this, the first print edition, from MadHat Press.

Apart from those works indicated below, to the best of the editor's knowledge the works appearing in *Shadows of the Future* are previously unpublished and appear at courtesy of their authors. Acknowledgement and thanks are extended to the editors of the following presses and journals:

David Chirot
"Torso" appeared on the cover of the chapbook *Pull of the Gravitons* by
    Marc Vincenz (Right Hand Pointing, 2012).

Carol Novack
"Same As" appeared in *Action Yes.*
"Mother and Daughter" appeared in *elimae.*
"Quanum Physics" appeared in *BLIP.*

JP Reese
"Midlife" and "Evanescence" appeared in *Mad Hatters' Review.*
"Play" appeared in *Camroc Press Review.*
"Release" appeared in *Used Furniture Review.*

Sarah Sarai
"The Quiet Softness" appeared in *Gargoyle*.
"Today No One Is Your Friend" and "The Philadelphia Art Museum:
      The Place of Weeping [Hafiz]" appeared in *Flâneur Foundry*.
"Look Now" appeared in *Scythe*.

Larissa Shmailo
"Oscillation" appeared in *Eleven Eleven*.
"Shore" appeared in *PoetryEtc*.
"Williamsburg Poem" appeared in *Soundzine*.

Jeffrey Side
"The Other Half of Her" appeared in *Mad Hatters' Review*.

Jürgen Smit
"Asemic Travel Journal 1854," "Book of Dreams (fragment)," and
      "Book of Dreams (fragment)" appeared in *Mad Hatters'*
      Review.

Marc Vincenz
"Imago" appeared in *Connotation Press*.
"The Uh-Huh" appeared in *Metazen*.
"The She" appeared in *elimae*.
"Swimming Sheila in Psychopomp" appeared in *Metazen*.

www.ingramcontent.com/pod-product-compliance
Lightning Source LLC
Chambersburg PA
CBHW031259090426
42742CB00007B/516